REDEMPTIVE
SUFFERING

Other Books by William J. O'Malley

Meeting the Living God
The Fifth Week
Why Not?
Daily Prayers for Busy People
Converting the Baptized
Building Your Own Conscience
Becoming a Catechist
Yielding
Why Be Catholic?
Clever Foxes and Lucky Klutzes
Dangerous Prayer
The Sacraments: Rites of Passage
Matthew, Mark, Luke, and You
Evolving a Soul

REDEMPTIVE SUFFERING

UNDERSTANDING SUFFERING, LIVING WITH IT, GROWING THROUGH IT

William J. O'Malley

A Crossroad Book
The Crossroad Publishing Company
New York

1997

The Crossroad Publishing Company
370 Lexington Avenue, New York, NY 10017

Printed in the United States of America

Library of Congress Cataloging-in-Publication Data
O'Malley, William J.
   Redemptive suffering: understanding suffering : living with it,
growing through it / William J. O'Malley.
     p. cm.
   ISBN 0-8245-1680-X
   1. Suffering – Religious aspects – Catholic Church. 2. Theodicy.
I. Title.
BT732.7.O68 1997
231'.8 – dc21   97-15540
                                  CIP

For
Mike Sehler, S.J.,
my brother and friend,
for
Cisco Dilg,
who posed me the ultimate question,
and for
the memory of
Bill Fold,
who showed me the answer.

The value of unmerited suffering [calls us] either to react with bitterness or seek to transform the suffering into a creative force. If only to save myself from bitterness, I have attempted to see my personal ordeals as an opportunity to transfigure myself and heal the people involved in the tragic situation which now obtains. I have lived these last few years with the conviction that unearned suffering is redemptive.

— Dr. Martin Luther King, Jr.

 # Contents

 # Acknowledgments

I once received a letter from a Spanish Jesuit in Bilbao. He informed me how profoundly he appreciated my book *The Voice of Blood*, about five Jesuits martyred in the late 1970s — so much so he had translated and published it. And "since everything in the Society of Jesus belongs to everyone else," he had done so under his own name. What could I do? Sue another Jesuit?

To avoid the same I must acknowledge I have been taught by, stimulated by, and perhaps have even stolen from authors I mention in the text: Shakespeare, Dostoyevsky, Chesterton, C. S. Lewis, Viktor Frankl, Rudolf Otto, Peter Kreeft, Richard Rohr, and many others — including Samuel Beckett, Albert Camus, and Voltaire, who taught me about the problem of suffering from a vantage point completely different from my own. I admit a debt even to my seminary professors who gave me prolonged lessons not only in rigorous logic but also in longsuffering.

But principally I owe a debt to Michael Leach, my publisher, who urged this bit of redemptive suffering on me at a time when, like Martha, I wrongly thought myself too busy about too many other things.

The Mystery
of Mom

My mother was in love with suffering, both enduring it and sharing it — in both directions. When she wasn't sick, or nursing some broken limb, or under an oxygen tent, she was an admirable, loving, tireless woman, working and providing a home for my dad, my sister, and me. She was profoundly religious, not only dutifully attending Mass, novenas, missions, even pilgrimages, but also open-heartedly welcoming stray girls whose parents had booted them out, cooking and baking to help out any family in the neighborhood with a new baby or a recent death. Wondrously inventive with cloth, beads, yarn, food, or anything else that came to her magic hands. Funny, a saltier wit than most sailors. And she was far more canny at business than my dad.

Mom had her faults which, like all idolaters, I was unable to discern, much less accept, until far later in my life. Neither my father nor my sister remotely lived up to Mom's expectations, all of which then focused like irresistible lasers upon me. To my benefit. To my anguish. And, after too many years, to my redemption.

When I was a boy, Mom was "away" for a while. There were whispers of something like a nervous breakdown, but I was too young to understand. Yet always there was something: broken arm, broken leg, her eyes, her woman's problems, and as the years went on and as I — her master-work — moved gradually further and further away to what might have been an independent life, the miseries seemed to metastasize. She had her first heart attack Christmas eve of my first year in college, and after that they came almost pre-dictably, year after year, especially after Dad died and I was in the seminary. And nearly always around Christmas, when (so that?) I would be summoned home.

For twenty-five years, at least once a year, I would get a call from a doctor saying my mother was in danger of death and I'd better come home. More than a few times, the doctors said the causes were psychosomatic. But the pain was nonetheless real. For both of us. Then after she'd had both hips replaced and could no longer stay either in the old house or in the one-floor apartment I'd gotten her (much against her will), there was the nursing home, where over eight years she gradually worked her way down from the fourth floor, where the patients were relatively capable, to the second floor, where the patients were scarcely aware they were alive or recognized anyone else. Including me.

I can't remember the year, but two or three years before she finally died, I drove from Rochester to Buffalo, where a mom who no longer knew me had been taken from the nursing home to the hospital. (God, this is painful to write, and Mom's been dead these fifteen years.) I had just come from saying Mass in a parish and mistakenly still wore my black suit and Roman collar. As I bent over the rails to kiss Mom, her eyes saucered in horror, and she scrunched over to the far side of the bed like a terrified scarecrow. "Aangh! Aangh!"

My heart clutched like a fist. And as I backed away, a nurse suggested I might better leave.

I groped my way down to the parking lot, sat in the car with my face jammed against the steering wheel, and sobbed. "God *damn* you," I prayed. "Why can't you let her go? Why can't you let *me* go? I've given you my whole goddamn life! Oh, maybe I've stolen a few pears now and then. But I've given you the whole goddamn *tree*, haven't I? Why? Why? Why? Why?"

And that's the ultimate question. Why?

One

Misleading Leads

It is easy to conjure up a God one can live with. The difficult thing is living with the one we have.

—Victor Steele

The Economic Metaphor

From the top, let's get rid of the biggest problem in understanding — even in an inadequate way — the roots of human suffering: the Church's ordinary, day-to-day catechesis.

According to the too facile (and therefore too frequent) economic metaphor, the primary cause of suffering and death is the "debt" incurred forever, for the entire human race, by the original sin of Adam and Eve. Our first parents flagrantly violated the one trivial condition imposed by an all-benevolent God who had bestowed bliss on them: They ate one piece of fruit from a forbidden tree. Because of that one act, God turned his back on them in an almighty snit and vowed nevermore to care for them till the last shekel of their debt had been paid centuries later in the blood of Jesus.

Further, he cursed them to labor under the burden of the day's heat, to endure menstruation, pregnancy, and child-birth, to journey through life never knowing when the next ambush awaited nor even whether they were headed in the right direction, and ultimately to face the inevitable and un-predictable fact of death, not only for themselves but for those in whom they had invested their love. And worse, that curse befell every human child born from that day for-ward: to grapple with "the thousand natural shocks that flesh is heir to," a sentence rooted only in their unwittingly having-been-begotten as human beings.

Thus, according to this catechesis, all suffering and evil — physical (earthquakes, plague, death itself) and moral (rap-ine, murder, thievery) — is rooted in moral evil: two humans' arrogant challenge to God's power, for which we all must pay.

Add to that primordial indebtedness the indisputable fact that each child of that original pair has reduplicated their ingratitude, over and over, for at least thirty thousand years. Oh, since Jesus, they are suffered to confess and be absolved of their personal guilt, *but* they still have to do penance in atonement, not only in this life but in some future purgatory, to expunge the nearly inexpungeable "temporal punishment due to sin," enduring agonies Dante delighted to detail — even after they apologized and were supposedly forgiven.

According to this widely held view, there is no way other than torment to appease God for being the progeny of such a pair — even though none of us chose to be born at all.

In the face of what Jesus told us of God, such a cate-

chesis is blasphemous. Even if it comes from a soul as august
as St. Augustine's. When Peter asked how often we must
forgive, Jesus told him not merely seven times but seventy
times seven times. If God requires such benevolence from us,
surely we can expect at least as much from an all-benevolent
God. Never once in the gospels when Jesus dealt with a sinner did the sinner have to grovel; never once did a sinner
have to give a scrupulous catalogue of species and numbers
of sins; never once did Jesus impose a penance, with the
one mild exception of the adulterous woman: "Avoid this sin
from now on."

If it comes to a choice between St. Augustine — or
the whole magisterium — against Jesus, I'll stick with Jesus
every time.

Such an explanation of suffering and sin makes a loving
Father into a vindictive Dickensian pawnbroker, immuring
sinners — and their families to the ultimate generation — in
a debtors' prison until the final farthing is paid. Such an inflexibly unforgiving God belies the entire Old Testament, in
which that eternally affronted God nonetheless stayed with a
whoring Israel for centuries. It also belies the fact that Jesus
swore in his inaugural declaration in the Nazareth synagogue
that he had come "to declare the year of God's favor": the
Amnesty of God.

But it is difficult for us (no matter what our attainment
in the Church) to comprehend amnesty: *unconditional* forgiveness. There's got to be a hook somewhere, surely. We
can't simply *accept* being *accepted*. We have to *pay*. Thus, even
after we have been forgiven, we must appease, atone, pay
back. And when those we love die and must face the excul-

patory agonies of purgatory, we feel we must give money for Masses which will somehow lessen our loved ones' "debts" and hasten their parole into paradise.

The minds that framed such a catechesis were the same as those that framed the Treaty of Versailles after World War I.

If that is a true picture of God, I pray I may never see that God in the face. If it is a true picture, there is little likelihood I ever shall.

Original Sin

Many find it difficult to read Genesis that literally. It insults intelligence to suspect all our woes root themselves in a pair of not overly bright nudists in a park, falling victim to the blather of a fast-talking snake. (Even Aesop, writing at about the same time as the writer of Genesis, didn't hope his readers believed there once was a time tortoises and hares actually made bets.)

Although the story of Adam and Eve never historically occurred, I nonetheless firmly believe it tells the truth: Even if you put two perfect human beings in paradise, sooner or later they're going to mess it up — making choices which any sane person would realize are ultimately not even in their own *self*-interest.

No matter what the *cause* of what we call "original sin" (our human penchant for screwing up), the *effects* are unarguable. One need only read any tabloid newspaper for proof human beings treat one another — and themselves — in a beastly, not in a human, way. The question is why.

Some sincere Christians believe the Genesis explanation of our origins as human beings is incompatible with the explanation supplied by the theory of evolution, which they believe must necessarily be godless. Not true, any more than communism need necessarily be godless; all vowed religious live in a freely chosen, godly communism.

Those comfortable with paradox find no reason why both Genesis and evolution can't be true — but each incompletely true, each needing the corrective of the other.

On the one hand, if no effect can be greater than its causes, the evidence seems to demand that intelligence in humans came from some intelligent source. One could not ponder the primeval laval muck and say, "Well, of course. Some day that writhing stuff will turn out Michelangelo and Shakespeare and Einstein." Some intelligent entity had to pre-exist and cause earthly intelligence; perhaps we owe our wits to some Frankenstein aliens, but we surely didn't derive them from King Kong.

On the other hand, the evidence seems also to demand that we yield to the truth that we have an amazing kinship with apes — even though our human potential exceeds theirs to an astonishing degree. The fossil evidence of humanoid development seems incontestable to any unprejudiced mind. We surely have evolved beyond our simian cousins — *but* without leaving our animal nature behind. At the root of our cerebral cortex is still a reptilian brain stem, wherein boil the same rapacious urges, angers, and territorial imperatives we observe in cobras, jackals, and sharks.

"Humanity" is a spectrum, an invitation to evolve into an ever *more* human self. Each of us has the potential, rooted in

our human differences from our animal ancestors, to achieve
the dignity and fulfillment of Joan of Arc, Abraham Lincoln,
and Helen Keller. Or we can content ourselves with simply
living upright, law-abiding, compassionate lives. Or, at the
bottom end of the spectrum, we can lobotomize our humanity, our souls, and live in total denial of our human potential:
pimps, pushers, terrorists, rapists, drive-by shooters.

Such unnatural people are human (simply because they
had human and not animal parents), but they are just
a hair's-breadth over the line from beasts, their human
potential undeveloped. They are what even the greatest philosophers wrongly limit human beings to: rational animals,
an uneasy fusion of computer and beast. What the definition
"rational animal" omits is precisely what makes us different
from any other species: hopes, questions, doubts, aspirations,
selfless love, creativity, courage, wonder — all the qualities
of the soul which are simply not reducible to the body or
the brain, both of which we share with beasts. The guards
who herded children into gassing stations in Auschwitz were
rational animals; they were not acting humanly.

Sit sometime in a zoo and study an old ape, our distant relative. Unless he is troubled by something outside his
smallish brain (fleas, hunger, the pheromones wafting from
the lady ape in the next cage), what does he do? He sits, gap-
ing at nothing at all. A sack of self-absorption and inertia.
Very little different from many boys I proctor in study halls.

There, I think, is the key to what we have always called
"original sin": the narcissism and resistance to change we inherited from our simian forebears, beyond which our human
potential invites us to evolve. But, unlike any other nature

we know of, humanity is precisely that: an invitation, not a command. Every other species' programming is irresistible. There is no bad rock, bad rutabaga, bad orangutan. Whatever they do, they're simply "doin' what comes natcherly." Only humans are capable of being "unnatural."

If God gave freedom to an as yet insufficiently evolved tribe of apes, moral evil — the suffering we inflict on others and on ourselves — was inevitable.

The root question arises again: Why did a good God do that? God did not create moral (humanly motivated) evil. But God surely gave us the tools to create it ourselves: intelligence and the freedom to use it harmfully, inhumanly, destructively. Why?

Physical Evil

If all efforts to get a benign God off the hook for allowing moral evil are ultimately self-deceptive, it is impossible to "absolve" God from being the root source of physical evil: cancer, misborn children, floods. Only the most fatuous would claim that, in each single case, God steps in and (for whatever reasons) says, "All right. It's time you contracted Alzheimer's." But it's beyond dispute that, if an intelligent Creator is responsible for the universe and all in it, that Creator freely chose one in which all those physical evils could occur.

The demonstrable existence of mindless suffering at least seems to argue *against* an intelligent Creator.

Yet the design of the universe seems to argue conclusively to the existence of a Designer: Everywhere the laws of physics are the same, but how can one get order and predictability out of an accident; how do you get "laws" out of "luck"? The human eye alone should convince all but the most skeptical that it could never have come about sheerly by accident. It has an automatic lens and bellows more sophisticated than any camera; it takes color pictures, in three dimensions, sixteen hours a day, and yet you never have to change the film or have it developed; very often when they're damaged, eyes repair themselves! Even Darwin found the eye a stumbling block for his assertions that everything evolved by accident.

Reflecting on our own intelligence, we can see something of the Intelligence in whose image it was made. Its functions are to examine, analyze, and then synthesize, determine things' purposes by the way they are made. Our intelligence is the urge to understand, to find meaning. Then intelligent beings must have purpose — even in our agonies. If there were no purpose, no answers to our ultimate questions, then why are we the only species cursed with a need to find answers that don't exist?

This is the question that tormented Ivan Karamazov:

Tell me frankly, imagine that it is you yourself who are erecting the edifice of human destiny with the aim of making human beings happy in the end, of giving them peace and contentment at last, but that to do that it is absolutely necessary, and indeed quite inevitable, to torture to death only one tiny creature, the little girl who beat her breast with her little fist, and to found the edifice on her unavenged tears — would you consent to be the architect on those conditions? Tell me, and do not lie!

In his admirable book *Making Sense of Suffering*, Peter Kreeft offers "easy answers" to the mystery of human suffering which are popular, simply because they are reductionist: They address a mystery one can only continue to probe and deflate it into a problem one can dust off and be done with. They accomplish this, as all reductionist theories do, by ignoring or evading or outrightly denying essential evidence which Kreeft sums up neatly in four apparently inconsistent propositions:

1. God exists.

2. God is all-powerful.

3. God is all-good.

4. Evil exists.

If you can just knock one of those assertions out of the equation, you might not be much happier, but you'll no longer be burdened by the "problem" of evil and suffering.

If you can get rid of God, for instance, the whole problem evanesces. No one is responsible. But also no one has a purpose for anyone's suffering. That's just the way things, meaninglessly, are. Noble souls like Albert Camus succumbed to that view and therefore saw all human struggle, all human dignity, as ultimately absurd. We are all on the *Titanic*, and there is only one direction we're going. Bleak, but surely possible.

If you can deny that God is all-powerful, you have the consolation of a caring Deity who really wants everything to come out right in the end, but who is helpless to intrude.

If God is not all-good, if God is capricious or indifferent or even evil, then there is no more value in trying to assess God's purposes than in guessing the motives of the weather.

If we could bring ourselves to believe evil doesn't even exist, that evil is no more than our fallible, subjective misperceptions of reality, then the problem would go away too.

If There Is No God

Thinking atheists are few; functional atheists who claim to believe in a "God" who is actually inferior to us are legion: "God is an idea that gives our lives direction and purpose; God is a feeling I get, like my conscience, to do right and help others; God is an ideal, the personification of peace, justice, and love; God is 'The Force,' the essence of energy that powers the universe; God is the summation of all the love in the world at any given time." Clustered among these fuzzy minds are the devotees of New Age mummery, the *élan vital* of creative evolutionists, and the Oversoul of Ralph Waldo Emerson.

In the first place, if what we call God is an "idea" or a "feeling" or a "personification," a result of human creation, then there is no God. In the second place, if God is merely an impersonal "Force," then to hell with it. The only way God can impinge on my life in any meaningful way is if I have some kind of *personal* relationship with God, if I not only can but ought to be grateful to God. I don't get up every morning and bow thankfully to the force of gravity for not having lost interest in me overnight and sending me sailing off into space. Gravity has no choice. God, if God exists, has to have — or be — an intelligence who can see alternatives and freely, purposefully choose among them. Otherwise the question of God and the mystery of human suffering are vacuous.

As we have seen, the evident design of the universe seems to argue to an intelligent Designer. Everywhere we look, each body is rotating on an axis and, in turn, circling around some other body, and that *pas de deux* moves around another system in a kind of cosmic dance. And if we go the opposite way and peer at a droplet of ditchwater under a microscope, we find the same damn dance! To say that such a complex — and predictable — system came about by sheer chance is as likely as dropping an atomic bomb on Mount Everest and expecting it to come down a working Disneyland.

I don't impose the periodic table on reality; it comes to me. There is order — out there; the rules of the dance are everywhere the same: the laws of physics. How do you get law and predictability out of luck? But there is also surprise! No two dancers are the same: spirals and rings, raging hot and rigidly glacial, smooth and pocked, positive and negative and neutral. This is not the dead movement of machine-tooled spheres but an endlessly varied carouse! There is not only an intelligence at work out there; there is also an imagination!

What's more, evolution at least seems to have a plan and a direction, from the simple to the complex. But in order for evolution to "work" without an intelligence requires us to "give" intelligence to entities which simply don't have it. In *Cosmos* Carl Sagan does that, at least twice. In explaining the quantum leap from inanimate to animate matter, for instance, he's forced to say that "one day, quite by accident, a molecule arose that was able to make crude copies of itself." When I read that, I wrote right in the margin, "That was one bloody clever molecule!" How could a brainless molecule discover anything? In speaking of the herds of trilobites which teemed on earth five hundred million years ago, he says, "They stored crystals in their eyes to detect polarized light." That "to" indicates purposefulness, but purposefulness requires intelligence. In the first place, how did those clever little trilobites know there was any light if they had no eyes? And what are those crystals they so shrewdly and deliberately stored? I find that when I'm writing at the chalkboard, an eye in the back of my head would come in rather handy, but despite all my degrees I can't for the life of me figure out what those ingenious but brainless trilobites did.

Less rationally but more tellingly, I find in myself certain specifically human hungers: for a reason to justify human suffering, for some kind of retribution for those who have been given a raw deal in life — and also for those who exploited them — and most profoundly I find a hunger to survive death. If there is in fact no one who has some (even unfathomable) purpose for pain, if there is no ultimate recompense, if we are in the end merely so much trash awaiting disposal, then Albert Camus is chillingly right: In a godless universe there are no greater curses than intelligence and hope.

Perhaps that is the truth. But I am then hagridden by a further question: If intelligence and hope are delusions, why are we the only species we know that is cursed with hungers for which there is no food? No sow snoozing in her ring of piglets has her dreams tormented by questions, doubts, hopes, fears. If there is no God, it would have been better to have been born a pig.

Reductionism is always appealing. It would be handy — however psychologically devastating — to factor God out of the picture. Unfortunately, an intelligent Creator seems to have left too many fingerprints.

If God Is Not All-Powerful

Rabbi Harold Kushner wrote a book called *When Bad Things Happen to Good People* in an attempt to understand the painful death of his young son, Aaron, as the result of a wasting disease. It is a testament to admirable courage, but its premise sacrifices God's power to defend God's love. His God is a victim of his own creation, shackled by its laws. There is no suspicion of the transcendent Yahweh, only a helpless benevolence. But a helpless God makes *me* even more helpless than I was at the feet of an omnipotent God.

I flirt with thin ice here, but I also sense the same (most likely unwitting) enfeebling of God in the present-day Church, especially in the liturgy. I find a God who only cherishes but doesn't challenge, Jesus the Warm Fuzzy, the Good Shepherd who tells us to "be not afraid" because he

will come to pat our wooly heads and make everything nice
again. Even the word "Kingdom," which Jesus used, is soft-
ened to "Realm" lest there be any taint of the despotic or
patriarchal. I don't sense the God-Man who cleared out the
moneychangers with nothing more than a handful of rope
and his own towering rage. I don't sense a God adept at spit-
ters and sliders and curve balls. I don't sense what Rudolf
Otto called the *mysterium tremendum* or the God John of the
Cross said we can meet only in "the dark night of the soul."
I don't sense a God before whom I must bow with Job in
grateful awe.

Rabbi Kushner's book sold in millions, all over the world.
Reductionism is always appealing. But it's a half-truth.
What it ignores is what Job discovered: God is not answer-
able to us.

When someone asks me, "How ya doin'?" I ordinarily answer, "Probably better than I deserve." Often they pull me
up short. "Of course you deserve..." What? I didn't deserve
to be born. I didn't even exist; how could I have *deserved*
anything? It's all *gift,* you see. Even the crap.

I did nothing to deserve good health or bad health, loved
ones or loneliness, perfect parents or flawed parents. I did
nothing to deserve life, much less a long life. To para-
phrase G. K. Chesterton, if Cinderella comes to the Fairy
Godmother, whining that she has to leave the ball at midnight, the Fairy Godmother could justifiably ask, "Honey,
who the hell said you could come to the ball in the first
place?"

God owes me nothing.

If God Is Not Good

In Archibald MacLeish's play *J.B.*, his modern interpretation of the Job story, Nickles, the fiery cynic who plays the part of Satan, chants: "If God is God, he is not good; if God is good, he is not God." What he's saying is that if the one we revere as the Creator actually is the one ultimately responsible for a world that could support Auschwitz and Hiroshima and the countless other torments the innocent must undergo, he surely can't be benevolent, and if he is in fact benevolent, he can't be in charge. It's that simple.

If God were out-and-out evil — if some sadistic Satan were God — then at least one could find a reason less nauseating than that there is no reason at all. But C. S. Lewis shows how that is impossible: "To be bad, [Satan] must exist and have intelligence and will. But existence, intelligence, and will are in themselves good. Therefore he must be getting them from the Good Power.... Evil is a parasite, not an original thing. The powers which enable evil to carry on are powers given it by goodness."

Or if God were merely capricious, like an omnipotent spoiled child, we might solace ourselves at least in some small way that we are victims, lifelong slaves incapable of escape. And many otherwise laudable believers treat God in that way: fatalists, who call everything God's will, even Auschwitz, even Hiroshima.

The point of Auschwitz and Hiroshima and other inhumanities is that, at the moment God gave humans freedom, God did not surrender omnipotence but God *did* surrender total *control*. That insight is crucial. No one —

not even God — can give another freedom which is genuine freedom, then step in whenever the decision is wrong, to rectify it with one's omnipotence. But God apparently believed freedom — freely putting part of his power into the hands of untrustworthy agents — was worth the risk, since without genuine freedom there can be no genuine love.

Just as Rabbi Kushner's heartfelt belief saves God's love by sacrificing God's power, the fatalist sacrifices God's love for the sake of his power.

But how could one surrender to a moral code supposedly written into the natures of things, which express their Creator's purpose and how they can legitimately be used, when that Creator himself is not bound by them? How can God expect us to be more forgiving than God himself is — or more compassionate? As I said before, if that is what God really is, I pray I never see that God in the face.

A more acceptable circumvention of God's caring, especially among intellectuals, is deism. Pondering the evident order of the universe, deists like the *philosophes* of the Enlightenment realized such a marvelously organized clock must have had a Clockmaker. But since such a perfect being, the Uncaused First Cause of the ancient Greeks, would by its nature be utterly unsullied, he/she/it would be beyond good and evil and surely incapable of involvement — or even interest — in such puny and soiled folk as ourselves. The deist God is an absentee landlord who set the operation spinning, then went off to some more diverting project. Others try to turn the mystery of suffering into a problem by making God a sadist or at least insensitive. Deism makes God absolutely indifferent to human beings.

If the universe were merely a soulless machine, if human beings were in fact no more than rational animals, deist reductionism would make perfect logical sense. But what it leaves out is too important. Peter Kreeft puts his finger precisely on their weakness: "We need more than a cosmic clockmaker to save us from sin, emptiness, loneliness, meaninglessness, despair, and death."

What's more, such a position ignores the numinous moments when we *sense* a presence more powerful than what we see — a sunset at sea after a storm, the first silent snowfall, the coos of a newborn child. What Hopkins called "the freshness deep-down things." Such flashes of unreasoned insight and delight snatch us out of ourselves (*ek-stasis*, ecstasy) because we were somehow caught "off guard." No one can force them; we can only be open to them. Awe is not simply an emotion; it's an intuitional insight into the aliveness of our context. Poet James Russell Lowell says:

> I remember the night, and almost the very spot on the hilltop, where my soul opened out, as it were, into the Infinite, and there was a rushing together of the two worlds, the inner and the outer. . . . I could not any more have doubted that He was there than that I was. Instead, I felt myself to be, if possible, the less real of the two.

It is easy for people to say such an experience is self-induced or hallucinatory, but then they have never had such an experience, most likely because they never allow themselves to be caught "off guard." And that is precisely their problem.

If Evil Does Not Exist

The question seems at first absolutely silly, as Voltaire showed so mercilessly in Dr. Pangloss in *Candide*, who asserted (while an earthquake destroyed thousands in churches on All Saints' Day, and his companions suffered betrayal, mass rape, and slaughter) that we live in "the best of all possible worlds." If God is omnipotent and omniscient, we couldn't possibly have it any better than we have it now.

Yet there is something to be said about this position. We do not see evil, any more than we see love. All we see are effects; then we argue to the cause. Thus philosophers like David Hume argued that what we discern as evil is really not an objective reality but merely the subjective reactions of the observer. Christian Scientists deny the genuine reality of the material world, believing that illness is a product of the mind which can be eradicated by prayer.

Idealism is but one more example of how philosophical systems can become enraptured with their own insights (which usually have some initial anchor in reality) and soar out into the empyrean like rockets on infinite trajectories, never bothering to check in with objective reality to find out if what they claim is still true — or important. I, who suffered seven years of scholastic philosophy and theology (in Latin) can testify to that. Communism has a valid point, and so does capitalism, but each needs the corrective of the other. As soon as theory lords it over the facts, the believer is in trouble.

A student once told me his teacher argued the idealist view very strongly, insisting we can never really know objective facts but only reflect on our unique subjective reactions to stimuli. I told him to give the teacher a good swift boot in the butt, and if the teacher reacted negatively, tell him calmly just to sit down and retool his subjective reactions.

Peter Kreeft tells an even better story. A son of Christian Scientist parents asked his minister to pray for his father, who was very ill. The minister remonstrated with the boy, telling him his father only *thought* he was sick, that his situation was an illusion based on his lack of faith. "Tell him to pray for faith." Later, the minister met the boy again and asked, "Does your father still think he's sick?" "No," the boy replied. "Now he thinks he's dead."

Conclusion

We can't fob off responsibility for suffering on a single mischoice of Adam and Eve, nor do we need to. Genesis seems right in presuming that, if no effect can be greater than its causes, there had to be an intervention by some intelligence if inanimate matter became empowered to grow, and then to move about and feel, and then be capable of rational thought. Conversely, from the evidence of all that's occurred since the creative Big Bang, it seems also clear God is "into" evolution; God is uncomfortable with status quos, with stasis. He seems more comfortable with *ek-stasis*. This is true not only of the entire macrocosmic universe but also within the microcosm of each individual human being. And evolution — growth — is suffering, at least in having to give up something we understand and are comfortable with to risk having something better.

Robert Frost once said that writing free verse was like playing tennis without the net. The same is true for the four reductionist attempts to deflate the mystery of evil and human suffering into a manageable problem. If the arguments presented here have been fair, we are left with the same question: How do we deal with lives in which both God and evil exist, and still believe that God is both all-powerful — responsible ultimately for all that exists — and yet also all-loving and purposeful.

It *is* a mystery, not a problem. You can certainly find some leads in your rational mind. But you will encounter the Answer only in your soul.

Two

The God of the Philosophers

Let me not pray to be sheltered from dangers
but to be fearless in facing them.
Let me not beg for the stilling of my pain,
but for the heart to conquer it.
Let me not crave in anxious fear to be saved
but hope for the patience to win my freedom.
Grant me
that I may not be a coward,
feeling your mercy in my success alone;
but let me find
the grasp of your hand in my failure.

— RABINDRANATH TAGORE, *Fruit-Gathering*

When I speak of "redemptive" suffering, I don't speak of redeeming myself from the anger of some insulted, punitive God. I speak of accepting — welcoming — the challenge of redemption from my own entropy, my own tendency toward ultimate inertia, redemption from my still-active animal roots. Every day of my life I want to be less like that old ape in the zoo, less like a bear caught helplessly in a trap, less like a steer plodding onward toward a death I can neither foresee nor find a meaning for. I believe that is what the Author of evolution created me for.

This chapter tries to face the mystery of suffering from the viewpoint of someone who honestly believes in "some kind of God" but has no strong affiliation at present with any religious denomination or tradition. It submits the questions to reason alone — and at least some tenuous faith — without reference to any institutional religion or scripture. However, I doubt it could do much harm to those who in fact have such a connection.

One day at the end of the first semester of my advanced placement English class — after we'd read *J.B., Oedipus, Grendel, The Once and Future King, King Lear, Candide, Hard Times,* and *The Color Purple* in an attempt to find hints at how suffering humanizes — a senior, intelligent and quite sincere, asked, "Why do we have to probe all these heavy questions? Why can't I just be content with my life?" He was asking, I suppose, why he couldn't just live a normal life, the way they do on sitcoms, able to cope with minor irritations but untroubled by the stuff of tragedies. Untroubled by greatness.

My first answer was simply, "Because you can't. Because life (fate, the gods, God) won't let you. Events over which you have no control are going to ambush you: floods, hurricanes, epidemics, the death of your parents, your friends, your child. And unless you opt to be a hermit, other people's agendas will undermine your contentment: drunk drivers, embezzlers, ambitious colleagues, fallible physicians, presidents who can declare war. There's no script, you see; it's all improvisation. What I'm trying to give you is some principles to cling to when someone unexpectedly and inevitably intrudes on your stage and derails your plot. That's a given. Like it or not, that's what life is."

If you had a choice of living an exciting life, a story worth telling, or a boringly secure life that would put any listener to sleep in five minutes, which would you choose? An exciting life, of course; you only go round once. But in opting for an exciting life, you're inescapably choosing one in which there are surprises, not all of them pleasant: ogres, dragons, fire pits, quicksand, and witches who have no discernible motivation other than delight in screwing up your quest. The only other option is merely to survive, to tread water, and tread water, and then die. Death — not just your own but the deaths of those in whom you've invested your love — is always inevitable and usually unexpected. Death short-circuits our complacency.

In order really to *live*, you have to be hyperaware, hypercurious, and hyperhumble before What-Is rather than What-Ought-to-Be. Even people who manage to live relatively unbothered lives miss out on their one chance to have a story worth telling. In *Our Town*, when Emily goes back from death to experience just one ordinary day of her life, she can't stand it — now that she understands what's really important. She asks the Stage Manager, "Do any human beings ever realize life while they live it? — every, every minute?" And he says, "No. The saints and poets, maybe — they do some."

If one's futile hope for life is simply to be unbothered, then the happiest human beings are in cemeteries. Yet many do have that unfulfillable desire. If that is true, then *everything* is suffering, even getting up in the morning, because it means leaving behind something warm and comfortable in order to find (one hopes) something better. As Carl Jung showed, anyone incapable of coping with *legitimate* suffering — rooted within the way things are — is headed straight into neurosis: anxieties, obsessions, narcissism, scapegoating, minimalism, masks, withdrawal, blaming our faults on our personalities rather than blaming our personalities on our faults. "I'm a procrastinator" seems self-justifying, as if it were an incurable disease of which I am a helpless victim.

But living an illusion, lying to oneself — and worse, believing one's own lies — is very hard work. Rather than face the terror of the dentist, we scrabble for over-the-counter palliatives that assuage the pain. For the moment. Thus we accept a substitute for the truth which becomes more painful than bowing to the truth. Rather than bite the bullet and purge the pain once for all, we let it drag on, and on. What's more, denying the suffering that comes from facing life as it is, flat on, avoids growth as a human being, since growth is by definition leaving the security of the cocoon in order to fly.

Legitimate Suffering

Aggravations arise simply from being an as yet incomplete human being in a world where the law is evolution and the lure is entropy, a tendency in both the physical and psychical world toward inertia. As Freud discovered late in his life, every society and every individual is moved by either one of two forces: Eros, the life wish, or Thanatos, the death wish. Eros craves challenge in order to grow; Thanatos craves the passive serenity of the womb, where we were warm, fed, floating, without a care, simply because we couldn't think. Either grow as a human being, or die as a human being — long before you have a flat EKG. Those are the only two options: evolve or atrophy.

Work is suffering: a loss of freedom for a felt purpose. Living with others is suffering: foreswearing independence, curbing resentments, compromising, because we can accomplish more together than alone. Wind sprints and weightlifting are painful but suffered for a felt purpose, athletic or cosmetic. Learning is suffering, disciplining oneself to persevere with few immediate rewards — which is why so little learning occurs, since those on whom it is inflicted find no felt purpose in enduring it.

Any significant change in one's life is, in its broadest sense, suffering: a loss. Growth itself is suffering, since we have to give up a self we were comfortable with in order to evolve a better self. But since we live in an ethos that recoils even from inconvenience, much less the troublesome effort to change one's stultifying habits, it is not surprising we live in a society populated in great part by terminal adolescents like Frasier. And those who control our society's Superego — the ad agencies and purveyors of entertainment and the big business interests which control them (and the rest of the world) — are eager to keep things that way. One can hardly blame them. They give us only what we want: to placate the Id.

Erik Erikson has shown that the human invitation is fraught with *built-in* disequilibriums, from nurse to hearse: crises which beckon us to a wider awareness and a deeper involvement in the human enterprise. Birth is a crisis, suffering: From a blissful existence as close to Nirvana as we will ever know in this life, we are ejected out into the cold and noise. But if we stayed as we were, we would die. And the first birthday gift we receive is a slap on the butt to make us cry. Or we never breathe.

For the next year or so, our parents try to accommodate our every need because, after all, we are still little more than animal cubs, "doin' what comes natcherly" — but with the uniquely human potential to become Martin Luther King, Jr., or Dorothy Day. Or not. But between the cub's contentment and human greatness lies a long road land-mined with challenges: weaning and potty training; separation from Mommy to play out in the cold with other snotty children; the traumatic abandonment at the kindergarten doorway; the atomic disequilibrium of adolescence and the struggle to evolve a unique self; the surrender of one's free-wheeling autonomy to join that self to another in marriage; the risk of having a child in whom one must invest most of one's adulthood (not to mention a quarter million dollars) — and sight-unseen(!); the inevitable challenge of aging, slowing down, losing the edge; and the final stage of human growth: dying.

It's all suffering. Either purposeful or purposeless. God, one trusts, has a purpose. The crucial question is whether each of us finds purpose in our suffering or not.

The Things That Can Be Changed

> God grant me
> the serenity
>   to accept the things that can't be changed,
> the courage
>   to change the things that can be changed,
> and the wisdom
>   to know the difference.
>
> — REINHOLD NIEBUHR

Too much of our suffering comes from denial that oppression can in fact be changed — if only with the self-confidence that undergirds courage. Fatalism is also a kind of neurosis, a sense of helplessness that leads to self-protective apathy.

In *Ordinary People*, Conrad Jarrett has just been released from a sanitarium where he's been as the result of a suicide attempt in grief and guilt for his brother's death in a boating accident, which Conrad — unforgivably — survived. His father has struggled helplessly to penetrate the boy's defenses; his mother lives in total denial, trying to keep up pretenses, struggling to remain "in control." Like Conrad, she knows that if she ever honestly acknowledges her feelings, everything will blow apart.

Reluctantly, Conrad goes to a psychiatrist, a loving bear named Berger who finally tells him, "If you can't feel pain, you're not going to feel anything else either." Apathy may not be the most dramatic form of suicide, just the most common.

So much of our suffering — or at least its intensity — is collusive; as Eleanor Roosevelt said, "No one degrades you without your cooperation." Subject someone to pressure long enough and he or she will either suffer emotional death (apathy) or dig in the heels and say, "This far; no further. I may not be able to stop you from hurting my body, negating my efforts, denying my worth, but I will *not* allow you to get into my soul." Often we subject ourselves to suffering which is in fact changeable — or at least challengeable, if only we could overcome our tactful and tactical caution, if only we could rouse ourselves to righteous indignation. "The fault, dear Brutus, is not in our stars but in ourselves that we are underlings." Of course at times rising against tyrants and petty martinets is useless, at times suicidal, but far less frequently than we fear. Perhaps we can't oppose an oppressor with rebel yells or muskets and barricades or even heated words, but we *can* oppose him — even if only in the silence of our own impregnable souls. Being quicksanded in collusive suffering can end *only* with an act of sheer *will:* "I *refuse* to be unhappy anymore; I will *not* let those bastards wear me down; I will *never* again let that sadistic cynic pierce my self-esteem."

Either that, or go on empowering them with your silence.

The Things That Can't Be Changed

At a workshop I gave one summer, one dedicated laywoman expressed her anguish over the fact that females are less than second-class citizens in the Catholic Church. I tried to tell her that even the majority of males are "powerless" in the sense she meant it: unable to act as ministerial priests, voiceless in Church policy. Even the great majority of clerics like myself are politically powerless. But she persisted, and her pain was profound and genuine. Finally, I tried to make her see that, at least for the foreseeable future, the ban on women's full participation in the life of the Church was one of the "things that can't be changed." The Vatican was in no way disconcerted by — or even aware of — her suffering; it changed nothing because it was checkmated from changing anything. The only one it ravaged was herself, uselessly. Sadly, she still couldn't accept that.

The first step toward genuine freedom is to jettison all the "if only's." Anything whatever that follows those two words is automatically futile. Impossible dreams are precisely that: impossible. Make peace with reality and get on with it.

You could say the same for sanitarium patients, amputees, victims of the Gradgrind educational system which functions merely as a series of holding cells, sorting the future workforce into managers and drones. They are in no way responsible for their existential situation. But they are responsible for their *attitude* toward it.

What do you say, for example, to committed religious who feel double-crossed by the universal Church, by their congregations, by their superiors, by their communities? Many live what Viktor Frankl described the lives of prisoners in the camps to be: "provisional existence of unknown limit." I think of this when, as predictably as morticians and the IRS, superiors get around (yet again) to the perennial problem of community. Their first "solution" is knee-jerk: We have to have more frequent liturgies; we have to have common prayer. They fail to realize that heartfelt community creates heartfelt liturgy, not the other way round. They fail to comprehend the impossibility of genuine community among people who have been *trained* to suppress their feelings, affections, angers — or who have smothered them out of gut fear they'll be hurt once again. ("If you can't feel pain, you're not going to feel anything else either.") You can't lobotomize thirty, forty, or fifty years of stifled bitterness, betrayal, loneliness, unshared pain. An impossible dream.

What hope can we offer such people — profoundly dedicated to service by ideals that surged in their hearts when they entered (or perhaps now stranded in middle age in a vocation from which they can no longer withdraw with grace), but left in the hands of CEO superiors dedicated solely to the institution's survival?

I defended myself from it for nearly ten years with habits, to the point that I resented any intrusion on my sacred routine even by something *pleasant!* Every weekend afternoon, for instance, I would have lunch, skim the paper, hang out with Jesus for a half-hour, then get back to work. One Saturday a wonderful Jesuit friend stopped me while I was reading the paper. "How'd ya like to take a walk for a while?" I paused, smiled weakly, cleared my throat, then finally said gracelessly, "Well, uh, sure."

It was a moment of epiphany for me. When we came back from our walk, I went out again to hang out with Jesus, and as I did I said, "I will *not* be unhappy anymore." That doesn't mean I'll be happy, but I won't connive in my own unhappiness anymore. I resolved then that I'd ask someone out for dinner every week, that I'd "waste" Sunday morning with the *Times* puzzles, that weekend afternoons would go just for fun reading. It's too bad we each have to find redemption alone, within our own telephone booths, but either we stand one by one or we all fall together.

Above all, you have to pray — not muttering prayers, not mumbling the office, but making an empty place in yourself and inviting God to fill it, connecting to God's energizing power, *feeling* that, no matter how indifferent those around you seem, you are never truly alone.

Richard Rohr has a story of a walleyed pike kept in a tank in an experimental facility. Every day, attendants dump minnows in the tank and — whump! — the pike scarfs them down. Then, however, the technicians put a glass down the center of the aquarium and dump the minnows on the other side from the pike. Whump! Whump! Whump! The pike smashes his snout against the glass, to no avail. He tries again, more listlessly. After a day or two, he gives up.

Then the experimenters drop in the minnows and pull out the glass partition. The minnows are right there; the pike sees them; but he "knows" they're inaccessible. The minnows flutter right up to the pike's jaws and gills. He ignores them. Finally, he dies. It's an object lesson Rosalind Russell often noted: "Life's a banquet! ... and most poor bastards starve themselves to death."

There is only one way out of a swamp. Out. If serving in the religious life is an integral part of who you are, then you have to *make* meaning, drawing it from the students, the patients, the clients, the manuscript. And God. Or starve.

Responsibility for Unmerited Suffering

Wisdom is making peace with the unchangeable. We have the freedom to face the unavoidable with dignity, to understand the transformational value that attitude works on suffering. Or we are free to struggle in panic, like a drowning animal, foreswearing our humanity. And not to decide in such a state *is* to decide.

Are we responsible for our unmerited sufferings? The answer is no. And yes. We aren't responsible for our predicament as its cause — whether it be cancer or joblessness or the loss of a child, just as we aren't responsible for our parents, the economic situation into which we are born, or our DNA. But we are responsible for what we do with the effects, for what we build with the rubble fate has made of our lives.

The only hand we have to play is the hand God or fate deals us. We needn't be victims of our *biological* fate. Stephen Hawking, crippled with Lou Gehrig's disease, is a good example of how a phoenix can rise from the ashes. Helen Keller was struck blind, deaf, and dumb, and yet through the feisty persistence of her teacher, Annie Sullivan, she achieved a breathtaking depth of spirit. Milton went blind, Beethoven wrote great music after he'd gone deaf, Dostoyevsky was an epileptic.

Only temporary greatness lies in the body; permanent greatness is lodged in the soul.

We needn't be prisoners of our *psychological* fate. As Frankl starkly and firmly asserts: "Faulty upbringing exonerates nobody." Those brought up in heartless homes are surely victims of others' misuse of their humanity, but it is an inescapable burden they were delivered, and they need be no more hamstrung by it than Abraham Lincoln was doomed by poverty. For those mired in self-pity, alcoholism, defeatism, there is a way out. They are free: to crawl ever so slowly toward the light or to wallow in darkness. Don't blame the System, or others, or God.

We needn't be prisoners of our *situational* fate, walled in by its "laws," living a provisional existence, settling for mere survival. People who went down on the *Titanic* went down singing. People have gotten off third-generation welfare. People survived Dachau, Auschwitz, the Gulag, Teheran, Bosnia because they knew (if only in their guts) that others can savage my body and even take my life, but they can't take my soul — not without my permission. If such heroism is possible for so many quite ordinary people, surely it's possible to say no to soulless societies and soulless selves, to Gradgrind, to the naysayers and nobodies we're surrounded by. Surely it's possible to say no to the values of the media.

There is a meaning to "value" here totally unfamiliar in a utilitarian society where "dignity, integrity, altruism" simply don't compute. What good is dignity when you're starving? What good is integrity when selling out will "save" you? What good is altruism when nice guys finish last? For those whose souls — their selves — are more important than their bank balances, or what others think of them, or even life itself, the fighting alone counts. There is no lost cause if the cause is just. In the going, we're already there.

Dying

Dying is the final stage of human growth for the individuals undergoing it, but it can also be a painful and growth-prompting disequilibrium for their caregivers and for those left behind. Because dying and death show us what's truly important.

Since the end of World War II, most children in our society have been cheated of the terrifying, puzzling, enlivening realization of death. Until then, the farm child — and even the city child — gradually wove death into his or her realization of life. Grandma was laid out in the parlor; Grandpa took a long time dying in the room behind the kitchen. Death was part of life. We assimilated into our souls the understanding that death was real. Today, death is trivialized on TV. Most children have witnessed more real and faked deaths before they reach kindergarten than a veteran in the army of Alexander. Conversely, *real* death is hidden away in nursing homes and hospitals: mustn't distress the young with the fact of death — thus depriving them of the chance to acquaint themselves with the real world in which they will have to wrestle for their adulthood. Most children I teach are spoiled — even the economically poorest of them. They believe somehow they have a right to uninterrupted happiness. Where they get that idea, I'm not sure. But they have it.

Negative as death is, accepting it has very positive effects on our lives. In the face of death, every other value lines up in proper perspective. Death shows us the worth of our days. Gold is precious because it's scarce; dirt is nearly valueless because there's so much of it. Our time — even if we refuse to acknowledge it — is precious because it is finite. There are a limited number of days I'll wake up, and therefore I'm grateful for every one of them. With an awareness of death, I find assaults on my bruisable ego much less hurtful. Eating crow and asking forgiveness becomes less distasteful because sometime it will be too late to say, "I'm sorry." Like suffering, death disabuses us of our pretensions to permanence and omnipotence. And death reminds us how fortunate we are to enjoy even what we've had and to express profound gratitude to the Timegiver.

With an endless supply of days, without death, nothing has any felt value. Even the gift of life itself. When one truly understands the meaning of death, it is easier to foreswear a claim to uninterrupted happiness and instead feel a sense of abject gratitude, like Robinson Crusoe discovering everyday objects among the flotsam on his island and understanding, at last, how precious they are.

After death, the agonies of the patient are over, but the suffering of the bereaved goes on. The family's suffering also has a purpose: It calls to us. We can babysit, force them to remain open, show up with food, accept them venting their anger, grief, pseudo-guilt at missed opportunities, help them readjust to a sense of "home" which has suffered a seismic shift.

What to say at a wake? Nothing. Surely not, "Oh, God has a plan." Only "You're not alone." That's all even God can say.

My Own Moment at the Pump

Helen Keller was, like most of us, blind and deaf to the really real. Afflicted in infancy, she grew up without knowing her family, without knowing what people were. She was the only person in her dark little world. After a while, she'd worked out a safe path through the house, where she knew by trial and error where harmful objects were, like stairs and doorways. Outside, though, was too big to plot a safe path through it, because the next step could be the edge of everything.

Then one day there thrust into her life the enemy of enemies, a teacher named Annie Sullivan, herself half-blind and Irish and damned if she'd content herself with just teaching this little animal table manners. She was going to crack open that safe, dark, self-centered world and let the great world come flooding in. For months they wrestled and punched and clawed, until finally Helen relented a little. She found it was more pleasant to be clean rather than dirty. When she was willing to eat with a knife and fork, Annie would let her eat. And always there was the funny game in the palm of her hand. Whenever her doll was put into her arms, four funny signs in her hand. Whenever she got a glass of water, five signs in her hand. Whenever the one with all the cloth around its legs came near (who was her mother), six funny signs. That's all it was: just a game.

Then it happened. Helen was out in the yard, and her shoulder hit the pump. She felt vibrations somewhere, and she was curious. She reached out her hands. They were wet. Something inside her was beginning to connect; something welled up into her throat. And from her mouth came the only word she could remember from her babyhood, before the darkness: "Wa-wa!"

It was the invasion. Suddenly Helen Keller realized that things have names! That there were other persons, outside her safe darkness, and she could communicate with them through the funny game in the palm of her hand. She ran to the one with all the cloth around its legs, and in her hand she spelled "Mother." Then she ran to Annie, and in her hand she spelled "Teacher."

Poor, frightened girl. She'd made the most liberating of all human discoveries. She'd discovered she wasn't alone.

Even those of us who are sighted are like Helen Keller in the Realm of the Really Real. God is drawing signs in our hands all the time, but like Helen we ordinarily bat them away, resentful of the intrusion and the resultant confusion. After a while, I think, God sometimes hauls us up short and shakes us good and hard to make us open our inward eyes.

God did it to me.

My mother was the last of ten children of a feisty and inventive widow in a small town in Ontario. She had to quit school after second grade to go to work, but she was intelligent and determined. When my sister came along, she was going to ride horseback and go to teas with white gloves. Unfortunately, Mom refused to yield to the truth; my sister was, indeed, a genuine duckling and not a changeling swan. She never got out of eighth grade, despite impoverishing private schools. My dad was, in my mother's eyes, at best an inadequate businessman. So when I made my appearance, after who knows how many miscarriages, I was a godsend not unlike little Adolf to Klara Poelzl Hitler. There was not the slightest whisper of possibility Billy might fail.

While most boys "proved" themselves at rough-and-tumble, I was pitifully un-jock, under strict orders from Mom ("You'll end up like a ragdoll in a wheelchair"). Instead, I proved myself with grades; never once in twelve years did I get a grade below 90. I brought home my first report card in freshman year (at a Jesuit high school, no less) with an *average* of 98. I kept it for dinner and passed it around with shy smugness. My dad said it was great, my mom thought it was wonderful, but my Aunt Grace (who wasn't my favorite relative in the first place), pursed her mouth and said, "What happened to the other two points?" It wasn't from my mother or father, but neither of them said, "Grace, shut your stupid mouth." So I went up to my room, closed the door, and sobbed. "What more do they *want?*"

Then, after two years at Holy Cross, I came into the Society of Jesus. In intelligence, I was now among the top 2 percent or so of men of my generation, but locked off in sylvan isolation, with no one less bright against whom to contrast myself. My grades (my sole norm for self-esteem, remember) began to sag, then waver, then plummet.

For seven years (interrupted only by three blissfully objective years teaching high school), we studied scholastic philosophy and theology. In Latin. There was only one comprehensive exam each year, oral, in Latin, in which three weird sisters sat balefully behind a table and could ask anything at all about what we'd "covered" in the last eight months. We were graded on a ten-point scale: ten was *summa cum laude;* nine, *magna cum laude;* eight, *cum laude;* seven was *mediocritas.* Now in Latin, that means "average"; in English it means something else. Six was *non superat mediocritatem,* in essence: "He can't rise to the level of mediocrity." Five meant you went into a slower course to become what we called jokingly "just a Mass priest" or what the more cruel called "ordained laybrothers." Kafka would understand.

For the first six of those years, my grades were: seven, six, seven, seven, six, *five.* I failed my first exam at age thirty-two, my self-esteem judged no higher over six years than, at best, *mediocritas.* And the Society of Jesus had become sort of an extension of my mother, only writ majuscule. My "mother" was saying, "You've failed me again and again, Billy, haven't you? Oh, Billy, I'm so disappointed."

If you don't succeed, you won't be loved. All love, you see, is conditional.

I carried my wretchedness around with me like an impaired child, agonizing over it, belaboring my friends with my unworthiness, my lack of ... everything. Even if I directed a wildly successful show, I could see nothing but the flaws. I told the spiritual father I felt like "a bucket of scum," and he said that, since my ordination was only a year away, I ought to reconsider taking such a huge step in such a state. I was, literally, suicidal. I stood one evening in a fourth-floor window, and the only thing that kept me from leaping out into the darkness was the hunch I'd probably botch that too.

Finally, one snowy Sunday in January, it came to a head. I had to make up my mind whether I'd order ordination invitations, ask for my parish church for my first Mass, or — my God! — tell *Mom* I was postponing what she'd awaited for twelve years: being the mother of a priest.

At noon I came out of the spiritual father's room after yet another go-round: "Yes, I should...No, I shouldn't..." Everyone else was on the way to lunch and then out ice skating, but I couldn't stand being with all those hatefully "normal" people, so I went back to my room. I paced, I fussed, I fretted. Finally, I said, "I've *got* to get away from this!" So I lay down, hoping I could fall asleep and at least be shed of it a while.

I didn't fall asleep, and the only way I know "it" lasted two hours was that I'd lain down at noon and came out of "it" around two.

It was like drowning in light. I was unaware of the room or of the time passing. But I knew beyond the possibility of doubt I was in the presence of God. And — diametrically against *everything* I believed about myself — I knew I was *accepted*. It was *beyond* the ideas and concepts I'd tried to wrap it in, that I'd been taught for years was the only legitimate "way through" to the truth. I was overwhelmed by it. Finally, I sat up and I said, for the first time in thirty-two years, without the slightest hesitation or qualification, "I'm a good man! And I'll be a good priest, because I'm a good man!"

Everyone else was back in the house by then, but I grabbed my skates and went down to the skating lake, and I skated round and round in huge circles, and I *shouted* it out: "I'm a good *man!* And I *never* have to prove it to anyone again!"

That's never left me. When I've sinned, when I've failed, I knew it was a good man who made a temporary blunder, someone worth picking up and starting over. It's why I'm a teacher, so the young people I teach don't have to wait thirty-two years to say, "I'm a good man," that they might have confidence — if not in themselves, at least in the One who approves and calls, the One who could make a universe out of nothing, the One whose Son could work miracles with materials as unpromising as mud and spit.

The first of the Twelve Steps is to admit you are powerless. I had refused to do that. True Pelagian, I had resolved nothing would prevent me from *achieving* God's love, the Society's approval, my mother's absolution. Now I knew, as Job knew, God — not a concept but a person who, no matter what my shortcomings, accepted me, with no ability — or need — to prove myself. Finally, I understood the crucifix: I conquer when I accept my impotence and am grateful for it, because then God can be truly God, and I can be truly me.

Since then, my favorite two lines in English poetry come from John Donne's "Batter My Heart, Three-Person'd God": "And I, except You enthrall me, never shall be free, nor ever chaste, except You ravish me."

It was the only way Mary could conceive the Christ within herself: allowing herself to be ravished. It's the same for us.

Bill Fold

One of the greatest human souls I've ever known was a fortyish merchant seaman with the improbable name Bill Fold, whom I met while I was a weekend chaplain at a terminal cancer hospital. Not only was he dying of cancer, but he had contracted tuberculosis and had to be kept in isolation. On top of that, he had a laryngectomy and communicated

only on one of those black-backed pads where the writing
disappears when you lift the waxed paper. One day, gowned
and masked, I said, "Bill, sometimes it must be very lonely."
He gave a small smile and wrote on his pad, "Yes. But isn't
it wonderful God trusts me enough to give it to me?"

That doomed seafarer, without benefit (or benightedness)
of advanced schooling, the Great Books, years of philosophy
and theology, in the crucible of his soul had laid hold on
what the great Dostoyevsky had discovered: "There is only
one thing I dread: not to be worthy of my sufferings."

We are never *driven* to moral behavior — to act humanly
rather than like a helplessly self-absorbed beast. One must
decide to have a personally validated conscience, ownership
of one's own dignity, a unique self.

Viktor Frankl, another purified soul, wrote:

> When a man finds that it is his destiny to suffer, he will
> have to accept his suffering as his task; his single and
> unique task. He will have to acknowledge the fact that
> even in suffering he is unique and alone in the universe.
> No one can relieve him of his suffering or suffer in his
> place. His unique opportunity lies in the way in which
> he bears his burden.

Metanoia

In explaining the construction of the well-made play, Aristo-
tle used the example of *Oedipus*. He says that at the heart of
every good play, the *peripeteia* (the turning point, the conver-

sion of the protagonist) coincides exactly with the *anagnoresis* (the acknowledgment of the inescapable truth). When, after struggling against the insupportable truth throughout the play, Oedipus the King suddenly comprehends his hubris, not in killing his father and marrying his mother, but in making himself equal to the gods, then his understanding of everything — everything — is *utterly* changed. He suffers a *metanoia*, not some embarrassed admission of some major truth-blindness clung to for a lifetime but an admission that he had been *totally* wrong, about the gods, himself, everything. A metanoia, a conversion, is a 180-degree turnabout, heading in the opposite direction.

The epistle to the Hebrews puts it starkly: "It is a dreadful thing to fall into the hands of the living God" (10:31).

We figure that if we — with some hesitation and trepidation — invite God into our lives, God is going to ask us to suffer some serious losses. As C. S. Lewis puts it, we expect God will come into our home and change the color schemes here, move the furniture about, break down a few walls. No. The real God — not the God of our hymns and homilies and holy cards, but the *mysterium tremendum* who rules in inaccessible light — is going to strip our home to the shell, shake it to the foundations. As Lewis says,

> You asked for a loving God: you have one. The great spirit you so lightly invoked, the "lord of terrible aspect," is present: not a senile benevolence that drowsily wishes you to be happy in your own way, not the cold philanthropy of a conscientious magistrate, nor the care of a host who feels responsible for the comfort of his

guests, but the consuming fire Himself, the Love that
made the worlds, persistent as the artist's love for his
work and despotic as a man's love for his dog, provi-
dent and venerable as a father's love for a child, jealous,
inexorable, exacting as love between the sexes.

If you wanted a different kind of God, you should have
arranged to have been born in another reality.

At the profoundest level, one "sets God free" to be God,
and loves the God we have — realizing always that genuine
love is *not* a feeling but an act of will, a commitment to the
beloved, come what may. We love God when we give back
the *control* God freely yielded us as human beings, when we
freely accept the invitation and challenge of being human in
a world that tries at every turn to dehumanize us. When we
say, "Thy will be done," we mean it.

Quite simply, we stop soliloquizing our miseries and yield
center stage to the Lead. T. S. Eliot describes it:

> No! I am not Prince Hamlet, nor was meant to be;
> Am an attendant lord, one that will do
> To swell a progress, start a scene or two,
> Advise the prince; no doubt, an easy tool,
> Deferential, glad to be of use,
> Politic, cautious, and meticulous:
> Full of high sentence, but a bit obtuse;
> At times, indeed, almost ridiculous —
> Almost, at times, the Fool.

The crucial point is that I *am* part of the cast. Somebody's
got to announce the duke, take the cloaks, tell everyone

dinner's ready — or else all the other actors will just sit there, unscripted, not knowing when to move or how to get offstage.

In the South Seas, whales are the messengers of the gods, as are eagles to the Lakota and angels to the prophets. For me, it's fat-bottomed black retrievers, more than once. One day I was ambling along a country road, hangin' out with Jesus, when just such a friendly emissary fell in with me. She had a stick in her mouth and kept hipping me to get me to throw it so she could retrieve it — which, after all, is what *she* was born to do. So I did, until my arm was limp as linguine, so I stopped. She came back with the stick and bumped me again, looking up bitchily as if I'd forgotten my place in the scheme of things. Just then, a car came screeching around a bend, and I grabbed her chain and choked her back till it passed. When I let her go, she growled deep in her throat and ambled away, looking back at me with an expression of utter rejection.

At that moment, I had an epiphany: I realized that dog understood my refusal to indulge her desires and my inflicting pain on her about as much as I understand God's refusal of my prayers and his visitations of unwelcome deprivation.

Long before Christ, Aeschylus wrote: "Day by day, bit by bit, pain drips upon the heart as, against our will and even in our despite, comes wisdom from the awful grace of the gods."

Now I believe that most often the wrath of God *is* the love of God, assessed by a fool.

Three

The God of Job

> *What is man that you should make so much of him,*
> *subjecting him to your scrutiny,*
> *that morning after morning you should examine him*
> *and at every instant test him?*
>
> —Job 7:17–18

Once upon a time, long, long ago, when God was still welcome in human lives (even in the good times), there was a man named Job, who lived in the land of Uz, southeast of Palestine. He was a prosperous potentate, blessed with a loving wife, ten children, servants, sheep, and camels. More importantly, Job was a "whole" man: blameless, upright, sacrificing daily to God in gratitude for his blessings and generous to a fault to those in need.

Meanwhile, at an assembly in heaven, God turns to Satan, whose task is to act as a kind of devil's advocate, a rather cynical prosecutor who espies human wrongdoings and reports them to his Master. God asks where he's been, and the

Adversary smiles, "Oh, around. Earth mostly." God smiles, too, and asks if the Adversary has happened upon his servant Job: "There's no one more dutiful and good than he." The Adversary snickers. "Really? Would Job worship you if he got nothing out of it? Job's worship is no more than insurance. Take it all away, and he'll curse you to your face." Sardonic, but still arguable. But God, confident in Job's loyalty, agrees to take up Satan's challenge.

In a single day, the sorrows come to Job in battalions. His oxen and donkeys are snatched away by a tribe of wandering raiders from the north; lightning strikes his sheep and shepherds and incinerates them all; Chaldean raiders steal his camels and slaughter his drivers. Finally a storm levels the house in which Job's children have been feasting, and they all perish.

Job tears his clothes with grief but refuses to lose faith: "Born with nothing, die with nothing. The Lord gives; the Lord takes away. Blessed be his name."

Then the Adversary afflicts Job's body with pustulant boils, and Job reels from his camp out to the communal garbage dump and sits there, wailing, scraping the ooze from his infuriating carbuncles with a potsherd. His wife, who has borne all these agonies too, but without her husband's maddening, impregnable trust, comes to him and screams, "Curse God! And die!" But Job says, "If we take the happiness, must we not take the sorrow too?" And his wife deserts him.

Job saw — at least before his friends diverted his focus — that we can't have happiness without sorrow, that either one is meaningless without the other, as inseparable as yin and yang, warm and cold, daylight and dark. Happiness is *not* a reward, and sorrow is *not* a punishment; each is essential even to understand the other exists. That truth is absolutely crucial.

There is a reason Job began as a potentate — as Oedipus and Lear were kings. They make clear that no one, not even the most privileged, is exempt from our common finitude and susceptibility to sorrow. The rich and powerful can insulate themselves from the common herd but not from our common humanity. Oedipus was a Greek, Lear a Briton, Job not even a Jew but an Edomite. No matter what one's rank or ethnic origin, we are all human beings: truly free, yet continually the subjects of passive verbs.

Then three of Job's friends arrive, Eliphaz, Bildad, and Zophar, learned in the traditions. They agonize over their friend's torment. They lament with him a while, then sit there with him, silent, for seven days and nights, sharing his grief.

Finally, Job speaks, bewailing the accursed day he was born. "Why let a man go on living in misery? I have no peace. My troubles never end."

At first hesitantly, then with the full ardor of the inflexibly single-minded, the friends begin to battle for Job's soul. For the next thirty-four chapters, the debate surges back and forth, each of Job's friends insisting that, no matter how egregious, his sufferings must be rooted in his sinfulness. But Job stubbornly maintains his innocence. Surely if he had committed some offense requiring suffering as outrageous as this, he would *remember* it!

Job's comforters were well-intentioned, like most fundamentalists, restorationists, unbending traditionalists. But they were like Peter in the gospel, full-heartedly trying to get between Jesus and his truth. At times they sound like insufferable academic prigs. They hadn't the slightest tolerance for ambiguity or uncertainty, unwilling to admit limits to their understanding. Worst, they insisted their retributive doctrine came from God's mouth. Job was fighting to keep believing God loved him — *against* human authority claiming to know God's mind. Therefore, Job treated God at times as if God were allied with these three: a Friend turned Enemy.

But to their credit, at least his "comforters" did show up, and they didn't knuckle under to Job's obduracy and leave him to his wretchedness. But Job's lifelong Friend, the Lord, doesn't show up for thirty-seven more chapters. That was Job's supreme torment.

In his anguish, Job shifts from spiteful to conciliatory to bitter to defiant to self-pitying. His wild fluctuations seem histrionic only to one who has never been betrayed in the depths of his soul by a friend.

At the core (or very near it) of the escalating to-and-fro in the Job dialogues is the error that Job and his friends argue about the *justice* of Job's torments. What they should be looking for is the *truth* behind them, which is quite another matter. Justice is what ought to be; truth is what is.

Another misdirection on the part of the friends was that they gave Job clear, rational, traditional, left-brain answers to what was, basically, not a left-brain question. What was at issue was Job's *feelings,* not just (or even primarily) his physical pain but his sense of betrayal by a Friend he had trusted for a lifetime. Jeremiah, chapter after chapter, echoes the same keening sense of faithlessness on the part of the One

we have trusted. But professional theologians aren't good
with feelings.

> You have seduced me, Yahweh, and I have let myself
> be seduced; you have overpowered me; you were the
> stronger.... The word of Yahweh has meant for me in-
> sult, derision, all day long. I used to say, "I will not
> think about him. I will not speak his name any more."
> Then there seemed to be a fire burning in my heart,
> imprisoned in my bones. The effort to restrain it wea-
> ried me. I could not bear it.... Why ever did I come
> out of the womb to live in toil and sorrow and to end
> my days in shame!" (Jer 20:7–9, 18)

But Job also made an error of his own, more subtle than
his friends' error: He maintained his innocence *as if God were
denying it*. Job overvalued his guiltlessness, turned it into a
bargaining chip. To the contrary, Jesus would declare: "When
you have done all you have been told to do, say, 'We are
merely servants: we have done no more than our duty'" (Lk
17:10). Martyrs suffer as a testimony to trust, even when
they don't understand (e.g., Our Lady at the annunciation,
Jesus in Gethsemane). And, from the beginning of the story,
God had known Job would not buckle. When the cynical
Adversary sneered at the outset that no one adores God
"for nothing," without hope of some reward, God knew Job
would stand faithful for a far different reason: love, loyalty
to a betraying friend, no matter what.

If Job had some hope of *ultimate* justice, his inner torment
might have diminished. But at that time, Hebrew theology
had no developed ideas of an afterlife, only a region called

Sheol, a kind of minimum security prison, like Limbo, in which wraiths drifted aimlessly about. Yet at least they were not in physical pain. But as Job says,

> There is always hope [even] for a tree:
>   when felled, it can start its life again;
>   its shoots continue to sprout.
> Its roots may be decayed in the earth,
>   its stump withering in the soil,
> but let it scent the water, and it buds,
>   and puts out branches like a plant new set.
> But man? He dies, and lifeless he remains;
>   man breathes his last, and then where is he?
>   (14:7–10)

What Job yearned for — what the bereaved at a wake or the patient coming out of the oncologist's office or the deserted spouse yearns for — is not rational answers but *empathy*, not only from their friends but from their Friend. Job felt God had deserted him, as Jeremiah and I — and perhaps you yourself — have felt deserted. When the Friend himself faced the end, he too cried out, "My God, my God! Why have you abandoned me!"

Ultimate Loss

Well into young adulthood, I had a recurring dream (for reasons which now must seem obvious) which mirrored an actual event in my childhood and which might embody the root of Job's agony. My mother worked with my father, and one day the young woman (shrew) hired to babysit me after school told me to go to the store. I suppose because I felt abandoned, unlike my Norman Rockwell peers who had mothers at home, for one totally uncharacteristic moment I rebelled and refused. The shrew called Mom, who had to drive home, harried, ready to crack, and for the only time in my life I was physically punished. She beat my legs with the razor strop.

In the dream, as on that day, I'm standing in the driveway, my face shellacked with tears, screaming without sound: "Mommy! Mommy!" And I'm running through lucite air toward the maroon coupe backing toward the street, my mother's grim face clenched above the wheel. She backs into the street and looks out the window, not at my face but at my feet. She shifts into first and moves away under the arch of trees. And she's never coming back.

I used to wake up from that nightmare with my face again shellacked with tears. I get the same grip in the guts when I read the story of the seven foolish bridesmaids and hear God growling at them (at me): "Out of my sight! I don't even know your name."

The ultimate, absolute abandonment. Forget Dante, whose hell is at least in a sadistic way interesting. Forget Sartre, whose *No Exit* is far closer to the truth, I suspect: three people who detest one another shut up together for eternity with no possibility of suicide or murder. Even that, however, doesn't capture the ultimate anguish: solitary exile in a featureless landscape into which Mister Godot will never come.

Theology and Tradition

Job's friends depended on theology, which is surely not a bad thing. But they depended on it exclusively: *external* authorities, hierarchies, dogmas, traditions. To understand the strengths and shortcomings of traditions consider Tevye in *Fiddler on the Roof.* The traditions of Judaism gave him and his family a sense of meaning and purpose, a matrix of customs and beliefs which sustained them against "the strangers' ways." But then his daughter imprudently fell in love with a Gentile, and tradition demanded Tevye treat this child he cherished as if she were dead. Tradition is important, but insufficient without flexibility, without common sense, without heart.

Job's friends drew on a retributive theology *about* God, but Job was depending on a relationship *with* God, which goes immeasurably beyond ideas, laws, concepts, traditions. They could weasel him out of his quandary only by appealing, basically, to the two lowest possible moral motivations: fear of continued punishment and hope of reward for capitulating. They were utterly incapable of comprehending one who has gone *beyond* conventional moral relationship; they couldn't fathom love.

Pelagianism is a heresy that got a name for itself in the fifth century but was actually the grandaddy of all heresies, in fact, the sin of Adam and Eve, which asserts human beings can, without the grace of God, achieve their own salvation. It holds that not only can we save ourselves, but we must. It resurfaced in pharisaism, which said, if you just kept the Law scrupulously, you could assure God's favor. It showed itself again in Dostoyevsky's Grand Inquisitor, who believed a hierarchical Church could relieve ordinary folk of the awesome burden of freedom — which requires what all humans recoil from: thinking for oneself. "Just do as we say, like good sheep, and all will be well with God." We can *prove* ourselves by our dutifulness and by our acts of reparation for whatever errors we've made. At rock-bottom, it's a belief our actions can *control* God.

Pelagianism — and Job's friends — simply can't bring themselves to accept *being* accepted. In my anguish about my unworthiness before ordination, I was a dyed-in-the-fibers Pelagian, convinced I had to *earn* God's love (my mother's, the Society's). Yet God loves each of us as helplessly as a mother loves her son on death row! That's a given.

This question of self-validation into which Job's friends steered him skewed the entire mystery into a problem of justice, which the foursome debated endlessly. Chapter 9 is full of it: "How can a man win a case against God? No man can stand up against him. He whom I must sue is the judge as well!" The odds are stacked against Job.

But that was the *truth!* The odds *were* stacked against him!

It's only when we yield to that humbling (for some, humiliating) truth that we can hope to be free. St. Paul said about the "thorn in his flesh":

I have pleaded with the Lord three times for it to leave me, but he has said, "My grace is enough for you: my power is at its best in weakness." So I shall be happy to make my weaknesses my special boast so that the

power of Christ may stay over me, and that is why I
am quite content with my weaknesses, and with insults,
hardships, persecutions, and the agonies I go through
for Christ's sake. For it is when I am weak that I am
strong. (2 Cor 12:9–10)

I no longer use petitionary prayers. For three years, I said
Mass for only one intention: that my mother be allowed to
die. And God did indeed answer my prayers. "No" is, in fact,
an answer. In that time, God painfully redeemed me from
the belief my prayers must, sooner or later, have an effect
on a plan whose scope my earth-bound mind is too puny to
comprehend. Now I pray as Jesus' mother prayed at Cana:
"They have no wine." She didn't say, "What are you going to
do about this wine situation?" Much less did she say, "After
all I've done for you, young man..." She merely expressed
her concern and allowed him to do whatever he thought fit,
without persuasion or even expectations.

When we let down our facades and share with a trusted
friend our fears, confusions, grief, anxieties, we haven't the
slightest notion (or hope) that the friend will "solve" our difficulties or make them go away. All we honestly look for is
a good listener, someone to share our weakness and lonely
bewilderment. God is an extraordinary listener; he rarely in-
terrupts. And his Son surely shared our weakness. Our prayer
will be far more beneficial if, like Job, we look not for solu-
tions but for a sense that, like Helen Keller within her dark
world, we are not alone.

When a child wakes from a nightmare, alone in the featureless darkness, she cries out in fear. Almost instantly, her

mother is there, flicking on the light and rocking her. "It's okay, honey. Everything's okay. Don't be afraid. I'm here." I think that's all anybody can reasonably hope for from prayer.

Job's Conversion

In chapter 19, Job comes to a resounding watershed in the debate, with an assertion which is probably the most frequently quoted passage from this book:

> This I know: that my Avenger lives,
>   and he, the Last, will take his stand on earth.
> After my awaking, he will set me close to him,
>   and from my flesh I shall look upon God.
> He whom I shall see will take my part:
>   these eyes will gaze on him
>   and not find him aloof. (19:25–27)

Note several things about this statement — which proves ultimately prophetic in the story. First, Job's trust in God is still unshakable, even as he is savaged by doubts, just as Jesus on the cross. Second, his trust is that somehow God will settle things *before* Job dies ("from my flesh," "these eyes will gaze"). Third, and most important, Job does *not* say, "I will finally know the truth and find satisfactory justice." Justice is a secondary matter, if only Job can reestablish the felt relationship with God which has always undergirded him.

Job's profession of faith has resolved his doubts, but it hasn't alleviated his isolation. He now focuses his attention on God's inaccessibility and remoteness; Job can't find *a way through* to God. He undergoes what John of the Cross called "the dark night of the soul," when everything in the soul craves union but God is — or profoundly feels — silently distant.

Simone Weil, quite likely a saint, but a woman unprepared to cross the line of baptism, wrote of it:

> Affliction makes God appear to be absent for a time, more absent than a dead man, more absent than light in the utter darkness of a cell. A kind of horror submerges the whole soul. During this absence there is nothing to love. What is terrible is that if, in this darkness where there is nothing to love, the soul ceases to love, God's absence becomes final. The soul has to go on loving in the emptiness, or at least to go on wanting to love, though it may only be with an infinitesimal part of itself. Then, one day, God will come to show himself to this soul and to reveal the beauty of the world to it, as in the case of Job. But if the soul stops loving it falls, even in this life, into something almost equivalent to hell.

Again, love is not a feeling; it is an act of the will, a commitment that sustains the relationship even when the beloved is no longer even *likable*. The profoundest love is the love of the mother of the death-row convict, the love of parents when their children say, "I've found someone I love more than I love you — at least in a different way," the love of the alcoholic's family, the prodigal love of the father for his runaway son, God's love for us when we say, "I don't need you," our love for God when God chooses to be silent.

God's "Answer"

Finally (after the hardly necessary intrusion of yet another consoler, Elihu), God shows up. In a whirlwind.

The unredeemed part of me always thought the whirlwind was a bit of a cheat on God's part, like the thunderous harrumphings of the Wizard of Oz terrifying Dorothy and her friends. But then I began to see it in the same light as the angels of Bethlehem singing their (non-existent) lungs out, the earthquakes at Jesus' crucifixion, the elegant brocades Renaissance painters bedecked Our Lady with at the annunciation: That wasn't what those people actually saw, but it sure as hell was what was *really* going on.

It is not God's orotund words — or the whirlwind — that count, but what the whirlwind *means:* God is overwhelmingly dynamic, untamable, the *mysterium tremendum* before which we quake, not with horror but with the same humbled fascination we'd feel before unspeakable power, vibrant yet controlled, equally intimidating and intriguing.

What the whirlwind "says" is: You can't capture this God in static words or well-balanced formulas or dogmas, whether the source is Augustine or Aquinas or even Teresa of Avila. Analytical, rational, left-brain arguments are important, but only halfway home. Other people's descriptions of their encounters with this daunting Personage are as radically uncommunicable as the reasons one loves one's spouse.

When you arrive at Job's situation, you have come to the foggy boundaries where incisive formulas have to yield helplessly to metaphor, when the only trustworthy pilot is

experience and gut instinct, not theory. There is only one
"way through" to God: meeting God, not in "fear of the
Lord" but in awe before the unutterable. It is like drowning
in light.

In the two chapters in which God first speaks to Job
(38–39), there is not a single answer. They are nearly all
unanswerable questions:

> Where were you when I laid the earth's foundations?
>> Tell me, since you are so well informed.
> Who decided the dimensions of it, do you know?
>> Or who stretched the measuring line across it?
> What supports its pillars at their bases?
>> Who laid its cornerstone
> when all the stars of the morning were singing with joy,
>> and the Sons of God in chorus were chanting praise?
>>> (38:4–7)

In effect, God was asking if he should check his plans
with Job before he executes them. Verse after heroic verse,
God questioned Job about the creation, the ways of the cosmos, provision for animals and birds, controlling the wildest
beasts. He even questioned Job about Behemoth (the hip-
popotamus) and Leviathan (the dragon), two chaotic, ugly
monsters who are nonetheless part of God's creation — with
no seeming purpose but to terrify. Yet God takes delight in
them! They, too, are an insight into the Creator's "personal-
ity." Can Job make pets of them? God can. With a majestic,
patient, ironic tone, God asked how Job could debate when
he was so ill-equipped for it.

God's "arguments" were no different from what Job's

friends — and even Job — had adverted to before (Eliphaz, 15:10ff.; Bildad, 25:26ff.; Job, 9:5ff.): that God's enormity places him beyond accountability to us. But it is much, much different here when Job *experiences* God's immensity, *feels* himself within a totally different, panoramic perspective — if not yet a transcendent one. (That will come in the next chapter.)

God's questions totally ignored Job's personal problems, and yet put them against a far vaster framework. In the end, Job didn't say, "At last! A teaching that makes sense!" He said merely, "I have seen you." He disowned his presumption and confessed that God's plans and purposes were infinitely beyond his understanding. But the dark night was over. Job had met God. They were friends again. More than enough. Friends puzzle one another, misunderstand one another, even betray one another. But the friendship is more important than its lack of logic.

At the very end, the fact God made the friends offer sacrifice in Job's presence while Job prayed on their behalf established that Job was right and they were wrong: Job was innocent, all along — which was never the point at all.

One final note on the story itself. Twice in his monologues God made the statement: "Brace yourself like a fighter!" (38:3; 40:7). It seems God is not only into order and surprise, but God enjoys feistiness as well as subservience. We find the same in Genesis 32, where Jacob wrestled all night till daybreak with a mysterious Stranger. Even though the Stranger had dislocated Jacob's hip, Jacob wouldn't let him go without a blessing. The Stranger said, "You will be called 'Israel,' because you have been strong *against* God."

And Jacob called that place Peniel, "because I have seen God face to face, and I have survived."

God doesn't mind our wrestling with him; that's why God gave us minds before God gave us authorities — just as long as we don't expect to defeat God, to comprehend God, to control God.

MacLeish's J.B.

In 1958, Archibald MacLeish wrote the Pulitzer Prize verse drama *J.B.*, recreating the most perplexing scriptural book squarely in the twentieth century, with Job's torments and tormentors very much events and people of our time. First, one son is killed in a war, by friendly fire — after the war was over; another two children die in a car crash; his smallest daughter is raped and killed by an addict in the back of a lumberyard; and his last daughter perishes in the rubble of J.B.'s bank, destroyed in some apparently atomic explosion which leaves Job devastated with radiation burns.

When his comforters come, they bring modern answers. One is a communist labor organizer who believes "one man's suffering won't count." But in the end history will inexorably bring "justice for everyone. On the way... it doesn't matter." For him, the triumph of "humanity" makes the individual's suffering negligible. A psychiatrist attempts to prove we are merely victims of our own subconscious drives and of events over which we have no control. Thus, we are nothing but victims; "guilt is an illusion." The final comforter is a hatchet-souled cleric, convinced like Luther and Calvin that human beings are from the very outset "bundles of corrupting bones, bagged in a hairless hide and rotting." What we must repent, he claims, is being possessed of a humanity we had no part in inflicting on ourselves.

When at last the voice of God thunders over the scene, Job in the play as Job in the Bible repents with the same words expressing his non-rational but nonetheless profound realization: "I have heard of thee by the hearing of the ear, but now mine eye *seeth* thee. Wherefore, I abhor myself and repent."

So far, so good. But it is not enough for MacLeish. While the pompous Mr. Zuss (who plays God's part) is sneering at the defeated fury of Nickles (who plays Satan's part), something is going on in J.B.'s mind. He raises himself up and says, slowly:

> Repent? For crying out? For suffering?...
> Must I be dumb because my mouth is mortal?...
> I will not duck my head again to thunder—
> That bullwhip cracking at my ears!—although
> He *kill* me with it. I must *know!*

He turns to Nickles, who has told him the only response to the filthy farce of life is to sneer, and he rejects him. But then he turns to the orthodox Zuss and says:

> Neither will I weep among
> The obedient who lie down to die
> In meek relinquishment protesting
> Nothing, questioning nothing, asking
> Nothing but to rise again and bow!

We are a long way here from the Book of Job and its abject submission to the difference between God's ways and human ways. Like Carl Sagan, Archibald MacLeish had a fierce intelligence; what neither could fathom was a profound and justified humility. Thus, when Job's wife returns, after an initial irritable reception (understandable with a helpmate who has screamed at him to "Curse God! And *die!*"), they join together to face the future, bloody but unbowed.

> We *are* and that is all our answer.
> We are, and what we are can suffer.
> But what suffers loves. And love
> Will live its suffering again....
> Over and over, with the dark before,
> The dark behind it, and still live, still love.

Although I fail to see a necessary connection between suffering and love, MacLeish's appendix to the book of Job ends there, a courageous affirmation of life worthy of the noblest Stoic. But one suspects, in any further conflicts MacLeish's Job and his wife will undergo, God will have very little role to play. It is a secular affirmation that human life and human love are the only props and rationale of bewildered humanity. In effect, the God of the Job story gets told off and sent dishonorably into the wings by Everyman and his wife.

J.B. makes for overwhelmingly powerful theater (despite a fondness for indecipherable sibylline clusters of words). It drew audiences one could hope for only with storybook musicals, and its literate audiences probably left the theater believing they had seen something "like, I mean, really profound."

What they heard was exactly the same reductionist message offered us by Matthew Arnold seventy years before in "Dover Beach":

> Ah, love, let us be true
> To one another! for the world, which seems
> To lie before us like a land of dreams,
> So various, so beautiful, so new,
> Hath really neither joy, nor love, nor light,
> Nor certitude, nor peace, nor hope for pain;
> And we are here as on a darkling plain
> Swept with confused alarms of struggle and flight,
> Where ignorant armies clash by night.

Of the four inconvenient premises we saw in the first chapter, MacLeish end-runs the mystery of suffering by denying the existence — or at least the relevance — of God. This is clear from a sonnet MacLeish published in 1926 called "The End of the World." In the octave, he describes a circus filled with grotesques. Then, just before the sestet, he writes:

> Quite unexpectedly the top blew off:
> And there, there overhead, there, there hung over
> Those thousands of white faces, those dazed eyes,
> There in the starless dark, the poise, the hover,
> There with vast wings across the cancelled skies,
> There in the sudden blackness the black pall
> Of nothing, nothing, nothing — nothing at all.

J.B. takes place in just such a circus tent, and the voice of God (the Prompter) has been an illusion all along. It is as

if the parable of the prodigal son had been reinterpreted by
Jean-Paul Sartre.

God: A Biography

In another Pulitzer Prize winner, *God: A Biography*, Jack
Miles takes much the same position as MacLeish. He ac-
cuses the Lord of the Whirlwind of invoking a Nietzschean
"might makes right" stance, a sheer amoral power. Yet I have
difficulty using the word "moral" about God, since I've always believed to be moral is to act humanly. But God is not
human. That's the whole point of the Book of Job.

Miles argues, justly, that "silence can be defiant as well as
deferential," and with intricate biblical scholarship makes a
case that Job's two responses to God are in fact refusals to
respond. This is in effect the same reaction as in MacLeish's
J.B.: a grudging, irritable surrender to power, as one might
accede to a concentration camp Kapo. "A man with [Job's]
linguistic resources would not be so brief," Miles says. True,
unless he were tongue-tied in awe.

I would argue that Miles might be like an actor search-
ing the script for a subtext to manipulate his role into the
lead, as if the play were about Polonius and not about the
irritating Prince. That way, the actor playing Job can pretend
to grovel in such a way that the (scholarly) audience can see
him covertly firing the finger at the Intruder.

Also, in his elegant culling of the Hebrew text, he seems
too earnestly attentive to the trees, missing the evident forest.
He seems incapable of the willing suspension of disbelief

that suppresses the suggestion: "Surely in twenty years of sleeping together, Jocaste *must* have said, 'Oedipus, dear, where did you get those interesting scars on your ankles.'" He forgets the book wasn't written for philologists but for ordinary folks.

One could wonder if Miles has never been cut off at the knees by the Lord of the Whirlwind and tried to make peace with his power, since the only alternative is accepting the total absurdity of human life.

Mystery

Any person is a mystery for which we have only scarcely comprehensive clues. God is no different, except in scope. A reductionist stereotype might help for a while in groping toward a clearer understanding of any person, but by no means a satisfying answer. Even a year's notes by a psychiatrist about a patient no more captures that person than a plot summary is the play.

Job's question is not a problem, but a mystery. Here we encounter again the difference between left-brain answers and right-brain answers, between critics and poets. Kierkegaard wrote: "A critic resembles a poet to a hair; he lacks only the suffering in his heart and the music upon his lips." Left-brain analysis and formulations are invaluable, but they don't go all the way. They are like the essential but ultimately disposable first stage of a rocket. Once we have met the One who justifies all theologies, they are no longer needed.

All head-trip types swear fealty to Socrates, yet Socrates'

fundamental assertion was that, in the search for truth, we must confess before all else we are not wise; we must be *humble* before the complexities of the truth and before our own limitations. Such heady folk submit to that, willingly. Then they pontificate as if they hadn't. Humility is what Job's friends lacked, in spades. "There are more things in heaven and earth, Horatio, than are dreamt of in your philosophy." Or your theology.

Only the author knows the end (both the conclusion and the purpose) of the story. But I do not know the end (in both senses) of my story. Therefore...

"No! I am not Prince Hamlet, nor was meant to be."

Each of us wants our lives to be useful. But the indeflectable corollary is that in order to be useful, we must be used.

Four

The God
of Jesus

Have you got human eyes,
do you see as humankind sees?
Is your life mortal like mine,
do your years pass as our days pass?
—Job 10:4–5

Job has a legitimate question for God: "Do you really comprehend what you're *doing?* You, who dwell in inaccessible
light! Do you have the slightest notion how it *feels* to be
bereft of everything — possessions, children, wife, respect,
health, meaning, even sleep? You understand suffering the
way theologians understand suffering, the way my solicitous
friends understand suffering. Do you know what it is to
grieve, to doubt, to *yearn?*"

It's a film cliché that some sympathetic helper approaches
a woman who's lost a child in some hideously unexpected
and unfair way and says, "I know what you must be going
through." And the woman snaps, "You *don't* know what I'm

going through." Only the sufferer understands — if "understand" is the right word. The suffering overwhelms body, mind, and soul, rendering the victim at least for a time incapable of anything more than *being* a victim, trapped within the incomprehensible.

If a purposive God is responsible for all that exists, philosophers and theologians insist that God must be perfect, not only without error or flaw but without doubts, without negative feelings, without the need or possibility of change: i.e., of growing, since growth would imply a lack, an imperfection. Homilists, catechists, and parents are thus wrong when they say our sins "hurt" God or make God "angry" or even mildly annoyed. The God who dwells beyond time, space, and need is not at all like the anthropomorphic Olympians: an overly inbred family seething with petty jealousies, intrigues, favoritisms, sexual obsessions. More than once, the Old Testament God says that although we may have some atavistic need to offer bloody sacrifices to placate him, he has neither a need nor a taste for them. If the philosophers are right, God is the quintessence of serenity.

Jesus changed all that. While remaining fully God, Jesus was also fully human. He experienced the stink of toil, fatigue at the end of the day, irritation at being misunderstood, anger at self-righteous hypocrisy, anguish at the loss of a friend. In Jesus, God *felt* deserted, betrayed, unjustly condemned, scourged, cursed, spat upon, felt his body invaded by thorns, nails, filth, felt his muscles scream in agony, his lungs fill with blood, his life drain away. In Jesus, God felt death.

For me, the profoundest attraction of Christianity is that

its God was tempted to despair, as I have been. As Emily Dickinson wrote, when Jesus talks of his Father, we feel un-nerved, "but when he confides to us that he is 'acquainted with Grief,' we listen, for that also is an Acquaintance of our own." Jesus erased all distance between God and Job.

There is only one question: How could a perfect being experience all that? That's a critical question.

Jesus' Consciousness of His Divinity

Something persnickety in us resents Jesus' divinity: "Oh, well it was easy enough for *him*. After all, he was God, wasn't he?" There are other trivial difficulties: When Jesus was no more than an embryo, was he running things from in there? When Joseph first took the boy Jesus into the carpenter shop, did Jesus just pretend he didn't know fifty better ways to make a chair than Joseph did?

But there are more substantial difficulties with a doubting, fearful, abandoned God. How could the temptations in the desert have been genuinely temptations — the kind we or-dinary folk contend with — when there wasn't the slightest possibility of Jesus' falling for them? When Jesus was sup-posedly in agony in Gethsemane, to the point he sweated blood, how could he possibly have hesitations about his forthcoming death if he had the full assurance of the divine knowledge and the perspective which saw this coming event in its precise truth: a momentary splotch of darkness on an infinite light? When Jesus cried out just before his death (at least in Mark and Matthew): "My God! My God! Why have you abandoned me?" was he just quoting a psalm to put the moment into perspective? Even worse, was he *faking* feeling forsaken? Those are not negligible concerns.

Less dramatic but more pertinent to our own everyday lives: on the one hand, how could Jesus be fully divine and yet doubt; on the other hand, how could Jesus be fully human and *not* doubt? Humans are the only species who doubt. No creek pauses to decide which side of a boulder might be the more advantageous; no carrot wonders if the soil might be better on the other side of the fence; no shark suffers pangs of conscience. Even angels (we are assured) never experience indecision, second thoughts, regrets. Surely God doesn't. Only humans. It's a constituent element of humanity that we must make decisions *without* certitude, commit ourselves on no better than calculated risks. That's what faith *means*.

I found "an" answer which satisfies at least me in the letter to the Philippians:

> His state was divine,
> yet he did not cling
> to his equality with God
> but emptied himself
> to assume the condition of a slave,
> and became as human beings are;
> and being as all humans born,
> he was humbler yet,
> even to accepting death,
> death on a cross.
> But God raised him high

and gave him the name
which is above all other names. (2:6–9)

At the moment of the incarnation, Jesus did not surrender *being* God, but he did — freely — surrender "equality
with God," that is, the use of divine power, especially divine
knowledge. Throughout his life, he insisted he didn't per-
form on his own but was an instrument of his Father's power.
"He emptied himself." If you will allow a crude analogy, the
second Person of the Trinity freely became "amnesiac" about
his own divinity. As a result, throughout his life, Jesus acted
on sheer faith in a God he had to try to understand with
human intelligence, just as we must. For that, his Father re-
turned him to his former place and gave him (back) "the
name which is above all other names": *ehyeh asher ehyeh,* "I
Am Who Am," Yahweh, the Lord.

so that all beings
in the heavens, on earth, and in the underworld,
should bend the knee at the name of Jesus
and that every tongue should acclaim
Jesus Christ is Lord,
to the glory of God the Father. (10–11)

Jesus always *was* God, but after his incarnation he had to
discover who God was and who he himself truly was, just as
every human must, step by step.

When Mary taught the child Jesus how to lace his san-
dals, it was new to him: learning. He surely was a very
bright boy, as witness his discussions with the Temple priests
when his parents had lost him, but he didn't necessarily have

some laser intelligence that cut through all uncertainties. The scripture itself says, "And Jesus increased in wisdom, in stature, and in favor with God and men" (Lk 2:52).

The critical moment — Jesus' own metanoia — came at his baptism by John at the Jordan when he had the thunderous realization: "Yes. You are the One." (In a far less significant situation, think of my encounter with God when I realized, against everything else I believed, that I was a good man.) Think of how dizzying a realization that must have been!

After that, the Spirit "hurled" Jesus into the desert, and his temptations were on *precisely* that insight into himself: "If you *are* the Son of God, turn these stones into bread; throw yourself off the Temple!" And those offers were genuinely seductive. In the first place, they were an invitation to this gifted young man to consider how utterly ludicrous such a conviction would be, a delusion of grandeur deserving seclusion in an asylum. In the second place, they did in fact make perfect sense, as any advertising executive would agree: If you want to change people's minds, buy their allegiance with bread, dazzle them with magic, coerce them with military power. This is precisely what Dostoyevsky's Grand Inquisitor castigated Jesus for: forswearing powers the Inquisition was not loath to accept and wield, out of charity for the simple and benighted, terrified of freedom.

But Jesus refused, daunting and enticing as the temptations were. He would trust the invitation of his Father, and he would refuse to usurp human freedom, settle for mindless conformity, yield the primacy of love over compliance.

His ordeal over, Jesus went to the meeting of the Nazareth synagogue and read the prophetic words of Isaiah, which defined the platform for his public mission, the foundation of what was to become Christianity:

> The spirit of the Lord has been given to me,
> for he has anointed me.
> He has sent me to bring the good news to the poor,
> to proclaim liberty to captives
> and to the blind new sight,
> to set the downtrodden free,
> to proclaim the Lord's year of favor. (Lk 4:18–19)

At his baptism, Jesus had indeed become "possessed" by the spirit of God; he knew — without the need or possibility of proof — he was the Anointed One: the Messiah. And the burden of his good news was freedom — not merely from physical poverty, captivity, blindness, exploitation, but far more importantly from destitute spirits, imprisonment in self-doubt, ignorance of one's goodness, submission to what can be changed.

"The Lord's year of favor" (Lev 25) was an ideal that, every fifty years, all debts were wiped out. It was, in effect, a universal *amnesty* — come one, come all; no strings, no retributive penalties, unconditional forgiveness. Jesus' mission was to give freedom, especially freedom from our "indebtedness."

Throughout his public life, Jesus' sole occupation was healing, forgiving, liberating from physical or spiritual enslavement. In the four episodes in which Jesus deals one-on-one with a sinner — the woman known as a sinner in the town (Lk 7:36–50), the adulterous woman (Jn 8:1–11), the Samaritan woman (Jn 4:4–40), and by extension the prodigal son (Lk 15:11–32) — in no case was there need to crawl, to vacuum the soul of every peccadillo, to submit to a retaliatory penance, much less "the temporal punishment due to sin" after an all-merciful God has forgiven. Unconditional amnesty. The *only* requisite in the moral practice of Jesus was admitting one's need for forgiveness. The only sinners Jesus was helpless to forgive were those who felt they had no need of it: self-righteous hypocrites.

The woman known as a sinner said *nothing*. She only humbled herself, weeping on Jesus' feet and wiping them with her hair. And all her unspoken sins were forgiven. To the adulterous woman about to be stoned, he says, "Has no one condemned you?" And when she says no one has, "Neither do I condemn you. Go away and don't sin any more." When the Samaritan woman says she has no husband, Jesus says (surely with a grin), "You are right . . . for although you have had five, the one you have now is not your husband." Then, without giving her a salutary talking-to, Jesus goes on to more important matters: having eternal life. When the runaway son returns to his father, he has a memorized confession all ready, but the father sees the boy "a long way off," which argues to the father's being out there every day, expectant. And the father runs to the boy, not the other way round, and the father forgives him *before* he can even get out his confession. For a "penance," the father gives him a party!

Despite his sinlessness, Jesus had a remarkable empathy for sinners and an extraordinary lack of vindictiveness. But most of us, addicted as we are to sick-sweet grudges, find amnesty — unconditional, no-strings forgiveness —

nearly incomprehensible. Yet that, in great part, is what "Christian" means.

If what I have said at least nudges near the truth, then Jesus faced challenges just as we must, with his wits, his evident humor, and his faith. It is difficult for purists to imagine the Son of God needing faith, but if Jesus was fully human, faith was one of his profoundest needs. That's why the gospels often picture Jesus going off alone to pray. When it came to the end, that's about all Jesus had left. Faith.

At the end of Mark's gospel version (the first written) of Jesus' agony in the garden, there is a puzzling event: "And they [his disciples] all deserted him and ran away" (14:50). But then in the very next verse: "A young man who followed him had nothing on but a linen cloth. They caught hold of him, but he left the cloth in their hands and ran away naked" (51–52). But they "all" had already deserted Jesus. Who is this other young man?

For a while, many believed it was Mark's "signature" (as Hitchcock made cameo appearances in his own films), but it is unlikely whoever wrote "Mark" ever was in Palestine or knew Jesus directly. Also, both Matthew and Luke had copies of Mark and were really writing new editions of his book, improved with new reported events and new insights. But they left out this young man, perhaps because it didn't make sense that "all" ran away but one was still left.

One solution is from the Greek Mark used. The English verb "followed" doesn't quite render Mark's verb *sunékoluthei*, really more like "shadowed," which is almost sinister. The Greek word *sindon,* a fine unused linen cloth, the adjective, *peribeblemenos,* "thrown about him," and the noun *neaniskos,* "a young man" occur again in Mark's gospel (and only in his). When Mark describes the women at Jesus' empty tomb, they are not greeted by an angel (as in Matthew) or by two men in white (as in Luke), or by two angels (as in John). They are greeted by "a young man," *neaniskon*, with a white cloth "wrapped around him," *peribeblemenon*. (The word for the white cloth is not *sindon*, but it is a white cloth nevertheless.)

The verbal similarities are too close for coincidence. In all four gospel versions the meaning is the same: The women encountered a "presence" (probably doubled in two cases because two witnesses were always required). Throughout both testaments, young men robed in white or angels are always used to embody the presence of God. Thus, Mark might well be saying that, after all Jesus' human companions abandoned him, even his sense of the presence of God sustaining him abandoned him! If that is true, then Jesus went through his passion bereft of the assurance of God's favor he had felt since his baptism. He bore all the agony with nothing more than guts and a faith he refused to surrender. Exactly like Job. Exactly like many of us.

Something similar occurs in Luke. At the end of the agony in the garden and arrest, Luke (and only Luke, 22:53) has Jesus say, "But this is your hour; this is the reign of darkness." That harkens back to the end of Luke's description of the temptations in the wilderness, at the end of which, "having exhausted all these ways of tempting him, the devil left him, to return *at the appointed time*" (4:13). Between those two moments, the temptations and the arrest, Jesus has been protected by a kind of force field, even against demons (whatever they are). But now, the "appointed time," "the hour," has arrived. The force fields are down. During the Last Supper, only Luke (22:3) says, "Then Satan entered into Judas, called Iscariot." Only Luke (22:31–32) connects Peter's denials with the Enemy's increasing power, readying for the kill: "Simon, Simon, behold. Satan demanded to have you, that he might sift you like wheat."

This is in fact the critical moment, the crisis. Just as in Mark, Luke's hero stands alone and naked before his enemy. This is not merely a conflict between an untamable rabbi and a handful of envious priests. This is a cosmic battle between the darkness and the light. And the hero will face it utterly alone, without even the sense of the protection of his Father.

In Jesus, God *became* suffering. Not an impersonal deist God, not some subjective God in our heads personifying goodness and love, not even the great energizing life force alive in the universe and its every cranny. But God himself was crucified, even teetered on the edge of despair with a plea *exactly* like Job's: "My God! My God! Why have you abandoned me?"

Teaching

In his apostolic letter *Salvifici Doloris*, "On the Christian Meaning of Human Suffering" (1984), Pope John Paul II wrote:

> Christ gives the answer to the question about suffering and the meaning of suffering not only by his teaching,

that is by the good news, but most of all by his own
suffering, which is integrated with this teaching of the
good news in an organic and indissoluble way.

Jesus faced the meaning of suffering in his teachings. He
did not hide from his followers the truth that they would
suffer not only the persecutions of Jeremiah but the physical
suffering of Job. "If anyone wants to be a follower of mine,
let him renounce himself and take up his cross every day
and follow me. For anyone who wants to save his life will
lose it; but anyone who loses his life for my sake, that man
will save it" (Lk 9:23–24). He promised them oppression:
arraignment before religious and civil authorities, betrayal by
their own kin, death. But "your endurance will win you your
lives" (Lk 21:19). "If the world hates you, remember that it
hated me before you" (Jn 15:18). The invitation to become
Christian, then and now, is not an invitation to a Sunday
afternoon ice cream sociable.

But Jesus also said to Nicodemus, "God loved the world
so much that he gave his only Son, so that everyone who
believes in him may not be lost but may have eternal life"
(Jn 3:16). For longer than I care to admit, I interpreted that
with childish literalism: "lost" equals "go to hell"; "eternal
life" equals "get into heaven." Rather I now see the Christian's task is to save souls from atrophy here and now and
to invite them to connect their spirits into the energizing
Spirit of God, not merely to ransom their days from stultifying routine but to live lives more alive than alive. Clare
Luce said, when she was considering conversion, she used to
look at believers and wonder, "You say you have the truth.

Well, the truth should set you free, give you *joy*. Can I see your freedom? Can I feel your joy?" Nifty questions.

Jesus gave a message about suffering also in the paradoxical beatitudes, which count sufferings as *blessings;* in his Kingdom, disadvantage is an *advantage*. But we've heard them so often we're no longer capable of hearing them. Perhaps they might take on new life if we looked at the negative instead of at the print.

"Happy are the poor in spirit," and cursed are those who can afford to sneer, who say, "I made something of myself, by God. Why can't they?" Their curse is their own smugness.

"Happy the gentle," and cursed are the macho, the cool, the invulnerable with their impregnable security. Their curse is their own empty eyes.

"Happy those who mourn," and cursed are those who never invested enough of themselves in others that others can cause them grief. Their curse is their own cramped asbestos souls.

"Happy those who hunger and thirst for what is right," and cursed are those who have nothing left to learn, no yearning, who are sated. Their curse is their own bloated emptiness.

"Happy the merciful," and cursed are those so sure of themselves they can cast the first stone, who thrive on grudges, who never forgive. Their curse is their own iron hearts.

"Happy the pure in heart," and cursed are those whose puritanism strangles the human spirit, the judgmental, the backbiters, the nit-pickers, who make us prove ourselves first. Their curse is their own passionless self-righteousness.

"Happy the peacemakers," and cursed are those whose hurt feelings are too bloated to swallow, who give no second chances — even to their own. Their curse is their own snarling edginess.

"Happy the persecuted," and cursed are those so lukewarm they stand for nothing, who refuse to stand up and be counted — and persecuted. Their curse is their own milky insipidity.

"Happy are you when they abuse you," and cursed are those so safe they have no enemies, that no one calls them "fool." Their curse is their own spinelessness.

There need be no hell for such people. They carry their hell within them.

The Passion

At the outset of Jesus' Passion, at the moment of his arrest, Peter — who had tried to protect his friend from suffering before — drew a sword and cut off the ear of the high priest's servant. But Jesus remonstrated with him again, "Put your sword back.... How would the scriptures be fulfilled that say this is the way it *must* be?" (Mt 26:52–54). Later, on the road to Emmaus after the resurrection, Jesus fell in with two disciples grieving over what they believed now a lost cause. "You foolish men! So slow to believe the full message of the prophets! Was it not ordained that the Christ should suffer and so enter into his glory?" (Lk 24: 25–26).

Of all the passages in Hebrew scripture, the most obvious reference here is to the Suffering Servant songs of Isaiah. If one knows the Jesus story first and only then goes back to read Isaiah, the references fairly jump off the page.

> Without beauty, without majesty (we saw him),
> no looks to attract our eyes;
> a thing despised and rejected by men,
> a man of sorrows and familiar with suffering,
> a man to make people screen their faces;
> he was despised and we took no account of him.
> And yet ours were the sufferings he bore,
> ours the sorrows he carried.
> But we, we thought of him as someone punished,
> struck by God, and brought low.
> Yet he was pierced through for our faults,
> crushed for our sins.
> On him lies a punishment that brings us peace,
> and through his wounds we are healed. (Is 53:2–5)

This whole matter of the scapegoat and atonement is, at least for me, problematic, and we will have to return to it. For the moment, I would call attention only to a few phrases: "ours were the sufferings he bore"; that doesn't really say he bore them so that we wouldn't have to (since we obviously still do), and "on him lies a punishment that brings us peace"; it doesn't say the peace is automatic, nor does it say that peace is the peace of being untroubled.

In John's description of the Last Supper, Jesus says, "I have told you all this so that you may find peace in me" (16:33). I don't think Jesus means the peace of the unbothered, much less the peace of the utterly uninterested or the utterly dead. I think Jesus means the serenity of tightrope walkers, of those who defuse unexploded bombs, of longtime terminal-cancer nurses.

In the Garden of Gethsemane, Jesus prayed three times: "My Father, if this cup cannot pass by without my drinking it, your will be done!" (Mt 26:42). Just as we must, the Greatest of Us struggled with his faith, because the purpose of his suffering was shrouded even from him. But he said — as we so often say incautiously in the Our Father: "Your will be done!" And Jesus really *meant* it. Even if that will were lacerating.

During his Passion, Jesus suffered most of the agonies and humiliations endured by concentration camp prisoners. Granted it was only for two days, but does a nun suffer rape more intensely than a lifetime prostitute? Does a child suffer torture more acutely than an aged professor of philosophy? Does a man who is convinced at the roots of his soul he is the Chosen One of God suffer more gravely than an ordinary innocent convict?

Jesus was betrayed by one of his own, humiliated and spat upon by ministers of his own religion, denied by his closest friend, shunted from the Roman governor to the besotted puppet Herod and back again, rejected by the people who had cheered him through the streets the previous Sunday — for a convicted terrorist, scourged with leaded whips, mocked all night and beaten and crowned with thorns by soldiers with nothing better to do, booted through the streets, his raw back stretched on the stony ground as his wrists were nailed to the crosspiece, pulleyed upward to hang for at least three hours. Again, he was mocked by sadistic priests shouting, "He saved others! He cannot save himself!"

In midafternoon, he cried out in a loud voice, "*Eli, Eli, lama sabachthani?*" that is, "My God! My God! Why have you deserted me?" (Ps 22:1; Mt 27:47; Mk 15:34). If what we have said regarding Jesus' understanding of himself is true, then Jesus has reached the depth of his agony here. Had he been deluded all the time? But just as at the agony in the garden, Jesus pleaded his cause but then yielded to God's will. Luke, the most sensitive of the synoptics, says: "Jesus cried out in a loud voice, 'Father, into your hands I commit my spirit.' With these words, he breathed his last" (23:46). Surrender. Without surety.

No reason the two versions of Jesus' final words do not harmonize. For a Jew of that time, the first line of a psalm triggered the *entire* psalm to those who had memorized it. And Psalm 21 ("My God! My God!") ends in a triumphant profession of faith:

For Yahweh reigns, the ruler of nations!
Before him all the prosperous of the earth will bow down,
before him will bow all who go down to the dust.
And my soul will *live* for him, my children will serve him;
men will proclaim the Lord to generations still to come,
his righteousness to a people yet unborn.
  All this he has done. (27–31)

One time during Easter week, a frighteningly intelligent little boy named Cisco, who had gone to all the Holy Week ceremonies, asked me, "Father, if God really loved his Son so much, why would he ask him to go through such an awful, awful death?" My only answer to him then is my only answer to him now: To show us how it's done. With dignity.

God will not step in and save us, any more than God stepped in to save his greatest love. As Bill Fold said, "Isn't it wonderful God trusts me enough to give it to me." To use another crude analogy, God is like a faithful father in the stands. He won't interfere, he won't harangue the coach — or the torturers. His presence, if we allow ourselves to contact it, says simply, "It's all right. You're not alone. I'm here. No matter what."

The crucifix is, indeed, a sign of contradiction. It captures, we profess, the most perfectly fulfilled human being who ever lived, at the moment of his greatest triumph, conquering *through* his impotence. ("My grace is enough for you: my power is at its best in weakness.") The crucial question to determine if one is a bona fide Christian is to look at that symbol and say, "Yes. I want to be like him." Now that calls for metanoia.

As George Macdonald wrote, "The Son of God suffered unto death, not that men might not suffer, but that their sufferings might be like his." And vice versa.

Completing What Is Lacking in Christ's Sufferings

St. Paul writes:

> It makes me happy to suffer for you, as I am suffering now, and in my own body to do what I can to make up all that has still to be undergone by Christ for the sake of his body, the Church. (Col 1:24)

That has always made me edgy, especially since other translations render "still to be undergone by" with "what is still lacking in." If Jesus was the infinite God (no matter what his awareness of it), his sufferings were objectively total. How can your sufferings and mine "make up" for what was supposedly lacking in Christ's sacrifice? Pope John Paul clarifies that:

Christ achieved the redemption completely and to the very limit; but at the same time he did not bring it to a close. In this redemptive suffering, through which the redemption of the world was accomplished, Christ opened himself from the beginning to every human suffering and constantly does so. Yes, it seems to be part of the very essence of Christ's redemptive suffering that this suffering requires to be unceasingly completed.

The "sufferings of Christ" are used here in two senses: the sufferings of the historical God-Man on Calvary, and the suffering of the new Body of Christ: the Church. Thus, Christ — in his extension in the Church — must go on suffering. Each of us must play his or her part in bearing our common burden.

The Jerusalem Bible translation makes that clearer than others: "all that has *still* to be undergone by Christ." The liberating insight of that passage is that the sufferings of Christ — the whole Christ, the Christ into whom we are invited by our baptism — did not cease when Jesus died. Christ still suffers, when we suffer, and — we trust — our suffering is redemptive just as his sufferings were redemptive. Not (as we will probe further in the final chapter) "buying off" a vindictive God, but redemptive in a far different, more positive way.

Remember, too, the passage from Philippians about Jesus' incarnation: He *surrendered* himself, gave himself up, not merely in obedience, as so many kindly theologians would say. No, in trusting *love*. Obedience is of the will; love is of the heart.

As Christ was witness on the cross to utter trust in God, so we, too, are called to empty ourselves and become *empowered* by our emptiness. As the Hindu verse says, "When you are hollowed out, then you will be full." Pope John Paul writes:

> If in fact the cross was to human eyes Christ's emptying of himself, at the same time it was in the eyes of God his being lifted up.... Paul writes in 1 Corinthians 2, "I will all the more gladly boast of my weaknesses, that the power of Christ may rest upon me."... In such a concept, to suffer means to become particularly susceptible, particularly open, to the working of the salvific powers of God offered to the humanity of Christ.

You will find no solace in the gospel, especially in the passion of Christ, if you are repelled by paradox. It's *all* paradox, an endless flogging of the truth: God's ways are not our ways. Happy are the suffering; if you want the first place, take the last place; if you want to find yourself, lose yourself; the *only* way to resurrection is Calvary; Jesus *is* "the way through"! Power is born out of weakness. The power of suffering comes from seeing — from *feeling* — that one is powerless alone, but far more important from feeling convinced that one is *not* alone.

God "answered" Job from the power of the whirlwind; Jesus answers us from the impotence of the cross. Put the question of your agony, doubt, bewilderment to Jesus. But don't go for your answer to Jesus quietly preaching the sermon on the mount. Don't go to Jesus riding triumphantly on Palm Sunday. Go only to Jesus on the cross. He can "answer" you only from there.

Five

The Enigma of Suffering

The fairest thing we can experience is the mysterious. It is the fundamental emotion which stands at the cradle of true art and true science. —ALBERT EINSTEIN

In World War II, the Allies achieved a major breakthrough with what they called The Enigma Machine, which cracked the Axis military codes. It was a misnomer, however, because an enigma is by definition an inexplicable situation. The German ciphers were not a mystery but a problem, ultimately solvable by mathematics and mechanics. Suffering is a true enigma, a mystery. We can probe it with our rational intelligence, as we can probe other mysteries: God, love, fulfillment, morality. If we are authentically human, we can't help probing them. But eventually our minds stray into fog, where there are no clear lines or directions. Our maps impose lines on a terrain which is, in truth, *terra incognita*.

From the start, I've expressed dissatisfaction with too handy rationalist reductionism in dealing with God and

suffering, which imagines God dealing with sin and suffering the way a rationalist would deal with ledgers. Whether
the assertion is that suffering is rooted in the debt of our
primordial parents or in the accumulated (and undeniable)
crimes, villainies, and inhumanities of the entire race since
the Cro-Magnons, I can't accept a connection between sin
and unmerited suffering.

I can't accept that Jesus submitted to legal murder as a
scapegoat to divert God's wrath from us. I can't accept a
God who waits like a kidnapper for a ransom to be paid.
I can't accept that when I hold an infant in my arms at baptism, I am in any way liberating someone (incapable even
of bladder control) from some millennial guilt. As a human
being, the child is sin-prone, yes; sinful, no. All such "explanations" are too close to the inane belief that if you step on
a crack or break a mirror or open an umbrella in the house,
dire reprisals await. Suffering has no more causal connection
with eating a piece of illicit fruit than it does with popping
open Pandora's box.

I can accept a strict causal relationship between the sin
of drinking to excess and the punishment of ulcers or cir-
rhosis. I can accept that cruel beating can result in a child's
death and that crime deserves punishment. I can even accept
that David's seduction of Bathsheba might have resulted in
a venereal disease (it didn't), but the seduction did not cause
the death of Bathsheba's child. Nor can I accept any (or all)
sin warranting *innocent* suffering.

But this hubristic dissent at least seems to place me
four-square in opposition not only to the Old Testament's
consistent teaching but to the gospels, to Paul, to the con-

stant teaching of the Christian Church, both Catholic and Protestant. Perhaps it might be time to gather firewood for the *auto da fé*.

Calvary as an Expiatory Sacrifice

No one can deny that the Church — from the very beginning — has taught that the action on Calvary was an expiatory sacrifice, offered to atone for the moral faults of the human race. As Avery Dulles clearly points out, it is the central theme of the Letter to the Hebrews, in which Christ offers himself as a single, once-for-all sacrifice for sins (Heb 10:12). Paul says we make amends in the blood of Christ (Rom 3:25); Jesus was "put to death for our sins" (Rom 4:25); Jesus is a sin offering made that we might achieve divine righteousness (2 Cor 5:21). The First Letter of Peter states that we have been ransomed "in the precious blood of a lamb without spot or stain, namely, Christ" (1:19). Matthew and Mark show Jesus saying the Son of Man has come "to give his life as a ransom for many" (Mt 20:28, Mk 10:45). In John, the Baptist points to Jesus as "the Lamb of God, who takes away the sin of the world" (Jn 1:29).

The expiatory doctrine was taught by the Council of Ephesus in the fifth century, reiterated by Trent, and reappears in many documents of Vatican II. Paul VI in his *Credo of the People of God* writes: "We believe that our Lord Jesus Christ by the sacrifice of the Cross redeemed us from original sin and from all the personal sins committed by each one of us."

More harshly, Martin Luther held even those who whole-heartedly embrace Jesus as their savior are not scoured of guilt; rather, the merits of Christ cover our hatefulness as snow covers a dunghill, so God chooses not to see it. John Calvin (to put it too simply) believed the question of who will be the elect and who will be damned was settled before any of us was born. Karl Barth, in the punitive tradition, wrote of Jesus: "He stands before the Father at Golgotha burdened with all the actual sin and guilt of man and of each individual man, and is treated in accordance with the deserts of man as the transgressor of the divine command."

Dulles offers several theories which try to cope with the meaning of the sacrifice of Jesus. One is of penal sub-stitution, which claims Jesus freely took our place, just as Maximilian Kolbe took the place of his fellow prisoner to be tortured. Another modern existential interpretation is that Jesus "stands as a symbol to instill in us a new conscious-ness whereby we are liberated from selfishness and anxiety and brought to 'authentic existence.'" (The air in those words carries away from my mind any semblance of genuine thought, like a renegade balloon.) Karl Rahner and others propose a third theory, which says the crucifixion (coupled with the resurrection) gives us a clear sign that God's fi-nal word toward human beings is not one of severity but of mercy. Dulles's own response is that Christ died as the head of his Mystical Body, not in substitution for us but in identification with us. Finally, liberal Protestant theology balks at accepting the Father being pleased by the torture and death of his innocent Son; thus they eliminate the di-mension of atonement and, in Dulles's words, "reduce the meaning of the Passion to its exemplary value. Jesus is seen as a paradigmatic example of patience in affliction."

Perhaps that latter interpretation is a "reduction," insofar as it renders the crucifixion not a dramatic expunging of human indebtedness for sin, but to my mind it does avoid making God look less forgiving than God expects us to be.

My difficulty with several explanations of the sacrifice of Calvary — and with the interpretations of it going back through the consistent teaching of the Church, the Fathers, and the evangelists themselves — is that they seem posited on a God who needs to be placated, who refuses to forgive without indemnity.

I'm not merely "uncomfortable" with a God who demands repayment for debts, since there is no conceivable way we could compensate God even for our existence. We can't "repay" God any more than we can repay our mothers for all the care they've given us and all the times we've taken them for granted. No doubt there is a hidden literalism in me that recoils at picturing God as a Dickensian moneylender bilked over and over by his human debtors, immovable until repaid. If that picture were true, how to explain God's unremitting loyalty to an errant Israel over the centuries? Even more disconcerting: How can anyone, even Jesus, placate a God who, by definition, can't even be upset?

I dare not say I "reject" the doctrine of expiation, but I find enormous difficulty with it, especially since I know Paul was wrong about both women and slavery, that Peter was not only wrong but clearly recanted his former positions on two elements of the faith he previously considered nonnegotiable: circumcision and the Jewish dietary laws. And I know beyond doubt or denial that the Church was wrong about usury, the Inquisition, and the crusades. I don't impugn the Church or tradition; I simply can't hold them to be unquestionably flawless.

I think, now, that's why I took on this book: to find a better — or at least less inadequate (not to suggest blasphemous) — understanding of unmerited suffering. I don't deny God exists or that evil exists; I don't deny God is both all-good and all-powerful. But I do deny God is vindictive.

Calvary and Vindictive Catechesis

Perhaps I can save myself from ecclesiastical prison (or worse) by uncoupling my confusion into separate questions rather than running full tilt at an amorphous uneasiness with what is certainly a crucial doctrine of Christianity. The first demon to exorcise is all elements of the question of redemption and Calvary that arise from the caricatures of catechesis — at least up to most recently. Secondly, I believe one can honestly separate Calvary-and-sin from Calvary-and-suffering, and also separate *both* sin and suffering from "the sin of Adam."

Since the quid-pro-quo economic metaphor for explaining Calvary is so deeply ingrained in those of us indoctrinated into Christianity (especially, alas, Catholicism) up until the 1970s, it is difficult to separate the legitimate insights of the Church we find in scripture and tradition from the well-meaning but inept and inflative catechesis most of us took as unquestionable as we underwent it: Fr. Arnall's apocalyptic visions of punishment in *Portrait of the Artist as a Young Man* (which many of us endured ourselves in retreats and missions), the grammar-school nun caricatures, the subliminal images of God as a Dickensian clerk, sitting with a huge ledger and ink-stained fingers at the top of a tightrope, just *waiting* for us to make *one...false...step*. We can chuckle at such absurdities now, but something in the gut still tightens without our wanting it to.

I think intelligent Christians can legitimately jettison the overkill of Dante and the Dickens-imitators as bogey men to terrify credulous children, exhume all the "divine" bookkeepers and pawnbrokers and ghouls from the dungeons of our souls, and send them on their way — in order to grasp a God who is beyond harm, beyond insult, beyond vindictiveness.

But there are also echoes of such a "God" in scripture (especially in the Old Testament) and in tradition: the concept of ransom and the analogy of the scapegoat. As you can see, I keep trying to understand things by analogy — the better known in some approximative way clarifying the less known. It's the way Jesus taught. But in the example I used (Kolbe taking the place of his fellow prisoner) or Sydney Carton replacing the husband of the woman he loved, the scapegoat came forward to face an *evil* repressor. At least as I understand it, the Old Testament use of the scapegoat — as well as animal sacrifice — was pure and simple to *placate*. That's where my thoughts snarl and analogy founders. The metaphor of the scapegoat, and to a lesser degree the metaphor of ransom, seem to "require" satisfying a *hostile* power. But in dealing with sinners, Jesus (the embodiment of God) never once required reparation, never once asked for a retaliatory penance. The prodigal father "punished" his son with a party! Jesus said he didn't come to destroy the Old Covenant, but more than a few times he didn't hesitate to correct it. "You have learned how it was said to our ancestors.... But I say this to you..." (Mt 5:21–22, 27–28, 31–32, 33–35, 38–39, 43–44).

In the face of far more important understandings I have of the nature of God, I must fall back behind the defenses of a cliché: Even in scripture and tradition, all analogies limp.

Calvary and Actual Sins

The only way to understand sin is in terms of a personal relationship. That, after all, is what "religion" means. If we are honorable, we feel a need to make amends for our real sins — *even though God doesn't demand it.* In a relationship between husband and wife, child and parent, friend and friend, we *want* to make amends, times when "I'm so sorry" is just not enough — even when the injured party is completely satisfied with that. We also need to "set things right" within ourselves, and it helps to add onto the apology a dozen roses or a box of candy or an invitation to dinner. God doesn't need atonement; we do.

Also, even if an offense is negligible in itself, it gains in enormity with the dignity of the victim. To resort again to a crude analogy: To lob a rotten egg at a pal in a schoolyard is trivial, but to lob it at the president at his inauguration or at the pope during midnight Mass is quite another matter — even if both president and pope giggle, wipe it off, and go back to what they were doing. What's more, consistent in-gratitude to Someone who's given us so much is an infinite affront — even if God doesn't "feel" infinitely affronted. I can accept Dulles's idea that, as head of his Mystical Body, Jesus freely undertook the burden of representing us in an infinite act of atonement, which makes forgiveness readily available to us, whenever we're humble enough to realize we need it. God doesn't need atonement; we do.

Given the difficulties with Freudian projection of the father image and the feminist animus to patriarchalism, consider the relationship between mother and grown child. ("Grown" child, because it's too easy to magnify a child's fear over trifling depredations, shuddering that Mommy might find out, stereotypical Irish-Jewish guilt.) To be a valid way to understand how betraying a mother's kindness is at least remotely analogous to our betraying God's kindness, how-ever, the offense has to be a genuine, serious betrayal of a relationship: embezzlement, selling drugs, bringing shame on the family in some way.

The trouble is, most of us are not noteworthy sinners. In my waning years, I have a hesitant hunch that God's be-trayed my expectations of him more often and more seriously than I've betrayed God's expectations of me. As Frost said, "God, forgive my little jokes on thee, and I'll forgive your great big joke on me." In childhood and early adulthood, I surely inflated my sins in my own eyes. Part of it was self-dramatizing, but I think also part of it was (in some perverse or atavistic way) to justify my belief that my comparatively paltry sins could be in some way responsible for the enormity of Calvary.

Like pain, genuine guilt expands to fill the size of the container. Some of us have, in truth, betrayed God's trust in ways where for at least a while we were totally alienated from God, yet were still accepted back — unconditionally — if we wanted to be. But it would be difficult to imagine anyone past adolescence who has not betrayed God's trust in some *serious* way — not mortal enough to sever all contact, but not trivial either. We need forgiveness, too. We need to confess and apologize, lest the pedestrian nature of our sins seem to absolve us rather than embarrass us. Even if we are not dramatic sinners, Christ said "I'm sorry" for us, too, and offered God a Gift in our name.

Calvary and Innocent Suffering

When asked, "Whose sins are responsible for this man's blindness?" (Jn 9:1–3), Jesus himself said the young man had been afflicted not for what he had done or his parents had done but "that the works of God might be displayed in him." At least in that one statement, Jesus seems to be severing any connection between sin and unmerited suffering. Jesus implies that there is a purpose in suffering, but the purpose is not punitive.

In the words of the International Theological Commission: On Calvary "Jesus allows his enemies to unload their resentment upon him. Returning love for hatred, and consenting to suffer as though he were guilty, Jesus makes God's merciful love present in history and opens a channel through which redemptive grace can flow forth upon the world."

Jesus showed us that, yes, the innocent *do* suffer.

But both Jesus and the Suffering Servant were not tortured and slaughtered as a kind of quid pro quo. They were rather *models* of bearing suffering: self-offerings, in love and trust. Both endured the sufferings that befall *all* human beings. They rescue our suffering from the meaninglessness which unmerited pain would have in the godless world of Beckett and Camus.

Jesus *did* bring about the redemption of the human race by sacrificing himself on the cross. As Jesus says to the Emmaus pilgrims: "Was it not necessary that the Christ should suffer these things and enter into his glory?" (Lk 24:26). The pivotal question is the meaning of "redemption" and "sacrifice," and the relationship between "suffer" and entering into "glory."

Jesus doesn't "heal" us. We don't just "tap into" Jesus and all's well again; say fifteen daily rosaries without interruption and you're safe because you have a Get Out of Hell Free card. Jesus' sufferings offer a *way* to healing. But *we* must walk it. Just like forgiveness, healing can't work unless we cooperate with it.

Therefore, at least as a point of argument, I'd submit that one can understand Jesus' statement to the Emmaus disciples without the element of atonement, without the connection between sin and suffering. "Was it not necessary that the Christ should suffer these things and enter into his glory?" The idea of necessity indicates the Messiah's suffering was essential in the plan of God, and there is a connection between suffering and entering into glory. Also implied in everything the gospel and the tradition hold about the passion is that Jesus' suffering was *for* us: "This is my body, which will be broken for you.... This is a cup of my blood.... It will be shed for you."

The suffering of Jesus was necessary to show us in an undeniably dramatic way how to face unmerited suffering, an example of dignity, trust, and love — even in the face of despair. He endured his Passion simply to show us *that's the way things are.* Suffering is inevitable in human life — a self-evident truth even no atheist could deny. What Calvary is saying is that there is *no* way to enrichment of the human soul other than through surmounting unwelcome challenges. That is the "glory": the superaliveness of the human soul inspirited by God, just as Jesus was, because Jesus was. "And I, except you enthrall me, never shall be free, nor ever chaste, except you ravish me."

Jesus invites us to let him redeem us from our own reluctance for glory, from the rebelliousness not only of our flesh but of our spirits, from our resentment that God is God and we are not. Precisely that reluctance, that rebelliousness, that resentment is the core of the Adam and Eve myth: "God knows in fact that on the day you eat it your eyes will be opened and *you* will be as gods, knowing good and evil" (Gen 3:5). The hubris of Oedipus, of Lear, of Hitler. And each of us. We are not such megalomaniacs as they, but we do spend much of our thoughtful lives second-guessing God: "Why me? Why mine? Why now?"

It is the most humbling of conversions: letting God be God.

Calvary and Original Sin

Here's where the fishbone snags in the craw. Once one demythologizes the Genesis story, to what event do we attribute the source of original sin? No sane person can deny its *effects;* as Malcolm Muggeridge said, it's the only doctrine you can prove from the daily papers. But what was the cause? To attribute all human susceptibility to sin, all responsibility for innocent suffering, death itself — physical and spiritual — to the mischoice of a *fictional* couple boggles even naiveté.

Original sin is connected further to infant baptism. Again, no problem with adult baptism releasing the candidate from actual sin. But from what does it release an infant? Positively, I can see it as an invitation into a new family, the Trinity Family. It surely is an invitation to live a life beyond the natural life. But I fail to see any real connection between infant baptism and sin. As I said, every child is born sin-prone, but in no way sinful, in no way "stained" for having been born human — especially since none of us asked for it.

Try as I might, I can't elude the analogy of being born with inherited diabetes. Except in relatively rare cases, God doesn't visit the sins of the fathers on the sons. If such occurs (e.g., child abuse), it wasn't God's doing but the father's doing; what's more the son is free to go against his "training."

Therefore something perhaps unredeemed in me bristles against any references — scriptural or traditional — to Calvary atoning for "the sin of Adam." Up to the 1970s, the non-theologian, thinking Christian accepted that as literal and a given. But how could Jesus have died to redeem us from having been born "poor banished children of Eve," if Eve was merely a character in a *symbolic story* embodying our penchant for sin?

No one can deny we have the God-given freedom to subvert God's plan, but to say "someone" (whoever) at the outset screwed things up so badly that God had to go back to readjust his plans seems to undercut the divine knowledge. I find no inconsistency (anymore) with God knowing we would screw up and *purposefully* allowing it — just as Jesus (even without the use of divine knowledge) knew Judas would betray him and Peter would buckle under pressure. Peter rose to the challenge; Judas didn't.

All but the most unbending will admit the Adam and Eve story never historically occurred. Nonetheless, like *King Lear,* *The Catcher in the Rye,* and *Who's Afraid of Virginia Woolf,* it still tells a truth: If you put two human beings even in paradise, they'll screw up; we are all *born* suckers for a sucker pitch. But, unfortunately, the story of Adam and Eve is one of the few stories in the Old Testament anybody really remembers.

Adam is never mentioned in the gospels, except one time in Luke where he is incidentally used as a referent for Seth, his son. Adam ("the man") is used only four times in St. Paul, three of which times I will examine here, the other later.

> Death [*thanatos*] came through one man and in the same way the resurrection of the dead has come through one man. Just as all men die in Adam, so all men will be brought to life in Christ. (1 Cor 15:21–22)

Hereditary death seems to be ascribed to our "incorporation" into Adam, into our being the progeny of a primordial sinner. But it is not altogether clear whether this means physical death or spiritual death or both. But the most unarguable treatment by Paul of what would later (the time of Augustine, 354–430) be called "Original Sin," is in Romans, chapter 5.

Well then, sin entered the world through one man, and through sin death (*thanatos*), and thus death has spread through the whole human race because everyone has sinned. Sin existed in the world long before the Law was given. (12–14)

For the next verses (15–21), Paul continues the antithetical parallelism between Adam, the cause of sin and death, and Jesus, the solution to sin and death, emphasizing that the power of the grace of Christ overwhelms the power of sin. But it seems to affirm, unequivocally, the existence of a "hereditary sin."

This was a novel scriptural doctrine. The closest to a clear enunciation of the connection between Adam's sin and death came in Sirach (190 B.C.E.): "Sin began with a woman, and because of her we all die" (25:24). But the first prolonged examination of the antithesis between the death-dealing Adam and the life-dealing Jesus is in these two segments from Paul.

This teaching on hereditary sin was discussed by two early Church councils but clearly stated by the Council of Trent in its fifth session (1546). Its "Decree on Original Sin" says,

Thus it must not otherwise be understood: Through one man sin entered the world, and through sin death [*thanatos*], and thus death passed to all men, in which [sin] all men have sinned.

I would call in question the emphasis the Church has put on these (only two) quotations from Paul, with yet a third quotation regarding Adam:

A woman ought not to speak [in assembly], because Adam was formed first and Eve afterward, and it was not Adam who was led astray but the woman who was led astray and fell into sin. (1 Tim 2:13–15)

I don't think I need to — nor do I care to — comment on that verse and its relationship to what has gone before. I love and revere St. Paul, but as with most of my other heroes and friends, I have no delusions about his being flawless. And one has to "forgive" Paul for not knowing what we now know about evolution, paleontology, and the symbolic meaning of non-historical stories.

If human sin caused human death, what caused the deaths of dinosaurs, trilobites, and pterodactyls? Physical death antedated human existence; therefore, humans couldn't have caused physical death. However, humans indeed *could* cause spiritual death, and it is from this death Jesus came to deliver us. Paul adverts to that in his fourth reference to Adam (1 Cor 15:45–49):

The first man, Adam, as scripture says, became a living soul [*psyche*], but the last Adam has become a life-giving spirit [*pneuma*].... The first man being from the earth, is earthly by nature; the second man is from heaven. And we, who have been modeled on the earthly man, will be modeled on the heavenly man.

Paul is referring to two quite different non-physical powers: *psyche,* the created soul which makes us human, more than merely animals, and *pneuma,* the uncreated spirit which offers us a share in the dynamic life of the Trinity, which makes us more than "merely human."

The Jerome Biblical Commentary explains the meaning of *pneuma* succinctly (79:79):

The Spirit is the Spirit of Power (1 Cor 2:4; Rom 15:13) and the source of Christian love, hope, and faith; it frees men from the Law (Gal 5:18), from "the cravings of the flesh" (Gal 5:16), and from all immoral conduct (Gal 5:19–24). It is indeed the gift of the Spirit that constitutes adoptive sonship (Gal 4:6; Rom 8:14), which assists the Christian in prayer ("pleading with us with inexpressible yearnings," Rom 8:26), and which makes the Christian especially aware of his relation to the Father. This power of the Spirit is not something distinct from the power of Christ: Christians have been consecrated and have become upright "by the power of our Lord Jesus Christ and through the Spirit of our God" (1 Cor 6:11).

In an earlier chapter, I wrote that if God chose to give reason and freedom (*psyche*) to an as yet insufficiently evolved tribe of apes, moral evil was inevitable. Apparently, God thought that worth the risk; otherwise there could be no genuine love. But in evolving beyond our animal roots, we did not leave them behind; lurking beneath our cerebral cortex is still a reptilian brain stem.

Just on a purely human level, that soul is an invitation to evolve into an autonomous individual who nonetheless interacts with other humans with justice and charity. Even decent atheists acknowledge that difference from lower species. But the soul, the invitation to evolve into a more and more human being, *is* an invitation which can be refused, as witness mob hitmen, pimps, and terrorists. Thus, as we've seen before, "humanity" is a spectrum ranging from Hitler, scarcely above the level of an animal yet with access to human cunning, to Thomas More, who would rather die than compromise his beliefs.

Again, still on a purely human level, being unevolved is not a sin; not evolving is. We are summoned by our God-given human nature, which raises us above brutes to overcome — not physical death (which is impossible, which anteceded Adam, which even Jesus couldn't avoid) — but *spiritual* death, the death of the soul, the psyche.

Even Freud, as we saw in chapter 2, said every human is subject to one of two drives: Eros, the life wish, and Thanatos, the death wish which craves being unbothered, unchallenged, unevolving — in a word, Eden. But that debilitating craving yields to the narcissism and inertia we share with beasts. *Dolce far niente* may be a nice place to visit occasionally, but it is a deadly place to live. Visit a prison and see proof.

Because of our residual animality, we're "grace-resistant"; there is a predisposition to sin (ungrowth or even regression) inherent in human nature itself: Original Sin! Contrary to Pelagius, who believed we were born innocent but corrupted by a sin-infected environment (cf. Rousseau and J. D. Salinger), the penchant for evil is bred in the bone.

What Jesus came to offer was redemption, not from "the sin of Adam" but from our unwillingness to respond to God's purpose in creating us, to the challenges of grace: to broader and more profound and nobler depths of living and loving. He came, as the crucifixion proves indelibly, not to save us from physical death — which is unavoidable — but from the death of the soul: Thanatos. And in opening ourselves to the fullness of our humanity, we have prepared a hospice for the *Pneuma*, the super-enlivening Spirit of God. Jesus is the final step in evolution, which began at the creation, a leap into the light of its Creator.

No one can deny that, by the very fact of being born, we are "condemned" to death — no matter what kind of lives we lead. I'd rather find several other ways to struggle with God's purpose in choosing a world in which we must die. For one thing, without death, nothing would have any felt value, which shows clearly in so many people who blind themselves to the fact of death. It shows, too, in the vapid souls who have never suffered.

Suffering as Grace

Although I have problems with a punitive, over-masculinized (in the Jungian sense) God, I also have problems with the opposite image of a "pushover" God. I have no difficulty

opening my mind to the "feminine" in God, the God who
cherishes. But I find that God of little help when I am in
anguish. What I need most at those times is, at first, cherishing, but then challenging. I have been purposefully hard on
over-feminizing God, especially in our liturgy and in scrupu-
losity over divine pronouns. The God such folk speak of isn't
the God I've spent much of my adult life making peace with.
If the gospel is predominantly about a cherishing God, why
is its most focal symbol a corpse on a cross? Resurrection
theology without the cross is a half truth, just as the Lamb
of God is a half truth without the Lion of Judah.

Using the Goldilocks method ("this one is too hard, this
one is too soft"), perhaps there is a way to the truth between the two extremes: a God inclined to "tough love," to
whom grace does not mean a gratuitous infusion of power
but an invitation to discover within ourselves powers we were
heretofore unaware of.

Grace isn't what I was led to believe it was, a sort of zap
of spiritual energy from God. Paradoxically, I've found grace
is not a "gift" in that sense. Rather it's a gift of *challenge:*
"Because you have been faithful in small things, I will put
you in charge of larger things" (Mt 25:21). The reward for a
job well done is two more jobs. If that is true, the sacraments
are not accepting a jolt of power (which most often we don't
feel), but rites of passage into larger lives.

Baptism isn't an influx of divine presence but the gift of
apostleship, and confirmation renews it; reconciliation is a
challenge to accept being accepted and to live a fuller life,
buoyed by the confidence that, no matter our shortcomings,
God has chosen us; the Eucharist is a reminder that, just as

Jesus broke himself up and handed round the pieces, so must we; marriage and orders are calls to a larger radius of awareness and involvement than one had planned; and finally the anointing of the sick is a challenge to dignity, to accept this suffering not as an occasion to be punished but an occasion to be proud. The sacrament of suffering is a grace-invitation to hope.

In my waning years, I've learned the crucial difference between optimism and hope. Optimism is bright-eyed expectation; hope is openness to whatever comes — betting irrationally, against the odds, on a noble outcome. Only the dull-witted live past forty still clinging to the optimism of Voltaire's Pangloss: "We live in the best of all possible worlds." Pollyanna after forty needs counseling. On the other hand, one can't live past forty without hope, the unexplainable conviction that reality must be richer than it appears. Optimism bets "the sun'll come out tomorrow, betchyer bottom dollar..." Hope denies Peggy Lee's plaintive, "Is that all there is? If that's all there is, my friends, then keep on dancing. Let's break out the booze and have a ball, if that's all... there is." There *must* be something more.

Not only did God, as he did with Job, trust Bill Fold ("Isn't it wonderful God trusts me enough to give it to me"), but Bill Fold also trusted God. Faith is hope is love.

Suffering need not be a negative experience but rather a positive one — an intimidating invitation to yet another conversion. Abraham, Jeremiah, Job, Jesus all faced that daunting request, and Simone Weil told what happens to the soul when it gives up loving in the dark night. If Jesus is the vine and we are the branches, we can expect the same pruning the vine received. But the vine and branches trust that the Vinedresser knows what he's doing when he prunes; the clay trusts that the potter has finer plans for it when he slams it back on the wheel. There is no way in the world to explain to a rationalist what supports that commitment. In Robert Bolt's *A Man for All Seasons*, Thomas More says to his daughter, Meg, "Well, finally, it isn't a matter of reason; finally, it's a matter of love."

Nietzsche said anyone who has a *why* to live for can endure almost any *how*. There is the why: loving trust in our Father. That's the grace the cross offers, the way to glory.

Metanoia

The biggest obstacle to genuine religious experience is second-hand knowledge of God, hand-me-down religion. Most of us have been baptized, but many of us have yet to be converted. What we consider here has nothing to do with catechesis or with mere education but with the *experience* of metanoia: a total turnabout in what we accept as the limits of the real, of what we mean by "value." Jesus said if you want the first place, take the last place. But how can that be possible (unless of course you're the only one in the race)? There are two races, headed diametrically opposite from one another: one leads to Beverly Hills, the other leads to Calvary. The difference is that stark.

When the gospels call us to "repent," they don't mean just a cataloguing of sins to confess. They mean an utter reversal of viewpoint, to see every reality, every value —

even suffering — in a totally different light from that of an unbeliever.

Conversion means first of all expanding the limits of what one ordinarily considers reality. We are so busy most of the time with work, marriage, children, bills, leaky faucets, crabgrass, and — when we do get time to relax — with the utter unrealities of the media, that we have little time to ponder the imponderables. We fail to realize that each of us is rotating at 750 miles an hour through the nearly infinite carousel of the heavens. One of Einstein's great contributions to human understanding was the great leap of imagination — not analytical reason — which led him to guess there are more than the four dimensions of time and space we can apprehend with our senses. Wherever you happen to be, most of the reality in the room is utterly invisible. We see only a tiny segment of the light spectrum; we have no felt awareness of the radio signals or neutrinos or muons and gluons zipping about, even through our own bodies. We don't really see one another, just other bodies, and from the way they act and talk, we make at best educated guesses about the real them: their selves, their souls. "There are more things in heaven and earth, Horatio, than are dreamt of in your philosophy."

Science says nothing can be faster than light. Yet science delights in playing "what if." Well, what if there *were* an energy faster than light? It would move so fast it would be everywhere at once. Like God. So dynamic it would be utterly at rest. Like God. And science now believes when it cracks open the last building block of matter it will find non-extended energy. Like God. $E=mc^2$ means matter *is* energy.

As Hopkins wrote, "The world is *charged* with the grandeur of God." If only we were aware of it.

Couple that modern insight with the insight of Exodus. When Moses asked Yahweh his name, he was asking for more than a label. For a Hebrew, one's name designated a role in the community. And God's reply was "I am who am." What is God's role? Existence. God is the pool of existence out of which anything that is gets its "is." Insofar as the power of God is immanent, God *is* the *anima mundi* (the world soul). When we react in awe to the numinous in nature, we react to the Source of its aliveness and energy: "the grandeur of God."

The philosopher Thales said, "Everything is full of gods." All round us, if we are aware, we find rumors of God. "Welcome strangers, for by doing so, some have entertained angels unaware" (Heb 13:3). Anyone we meet could be a signal of God's presence in the world. Finding them depends primarily on the openness of our perceptions of reality. But it depends also on recognizing that much of what we think important is, against the background of the transcendent dimension of life and death, trivial.

And the overwhelming insight for a Christian is that this electrifying presence, this *mysterium tremendum,* is our Father.

When we place our sufferings, however horrifying, within that energizing context, on the one hand, they shrivel to smallness, yet on the other hand they are imbued with that coruscating Spirit.

The Spiritual Exercises of St. Ignatius Loyola begin with "The Principle and Foundation," that is, the bedrock truths on which all human meaning and purpose are grounded. The first four words are quite simple: "Human beings were created." For a theist that is an palatable truism. Yet, like "thy will be done," they are burdened with unnerving truth. Accepting them is an admission I am not in charge; I am (more often than I realize or like to admit) the subject of *passive* verbs: I was conceived; I was carried nine months; I was born — without any deserving or cooperation on my part. But I don't *like* being the subject of passive verbs; I want to be in charge, to be master of my fate, I can take care of myself, "Don't Tread on Me."

The inescapable truth is I am not. I didn't make up the rules of the game; my ideas and choices must yield to Someone Else's ideas and choices — or I will never find peace. No one ever said the truth will make you feel good. Just set you free. Each of us is free, as Frankl said, to choose our own *attitude* to our agonies. We can face them with the brute helplessness of an animal, raging, trapped. Or we can face them as Camus did, clinging to the dignity of which only fulfilled human beings are capable. Or we can face them as Job did, cleaving tenaciously to unbreakable trust in a loving God. Or, now, we can embrace them as siblings of Christ, our suffering echoing outward beyond the limits of this skin, this life, into the life of God. Christ and we are suffering *together*, and our trust gives God praise.

The Elizabethan martyrs — both papist and puritan — went to their executions, almost without exception, peacefully, generously forgiving their persecutors in imitation of the same Christ whose example at his ending was, "Father, forgive them. They don't know what they're doing" (Lk 23:34).

From the rubble of the Coventry Cathedral, blasted by the Germans for no strategic gain whatever, church members built an altar of broken stone and charred timbers. Across its frontal are carved only two words: "Father, forgive."

Their motives were not rational, but in the context of the really real, they were eminently reasonable.

This of course requires establishing a felt relationship with God, through the suffering and triumphant Christ. The root of the word religion is *religare*, "to bind fast," as in "ligate." Thus any genuine religion has to be a felt *connection*; when we pray there has to be some inner conviction we are truly being heard and are truly listening. The best kind of prayer, without words or requests, consists merely in really *being-with* God. Some find images (real or imagined) helpful; others just feel their souls honestly connected to God. When I pray sometimes, I like to think I'm dealing with "a Person made of light," amorphous, leaking out through everything around me. But the absolute essential is the felt person-to-Person connection.

The Person we contact in prayer lives beyond the limits of time and space. What that God is asking when he waits patiently to be invited in is exactly what God asked Our Lady at the Annunciation: "Conceive my Son in you today." In a very real sense, we are assenting to the invasion of the tiny kingdoms of our souls by the inaccessible and incomprehensible energizing force of the Trinity. Then we can say with Paul, "I live now not with my own life but with the life of Christ who lives within me" (Gal 2:20). If so, then Christ suffers *with* me, and just as his Father turned Christ's defeat into victory, so will he mine.

As Pope John Paul II writes in *Salvifici Doloris:*

A result of such a conversion is not only that the individual discovers the salvific meaning of suffering, but
above all that he becomes a completely new person. He
discovers a new dimension, as it were, of his entire life
and vocation. This discovery is a particular confirmation of the spiritual greatness which in man surpasses
the body in a way that is completely beyond compare.
When his body is gravely ill, totally incapacitated, and
the person is almost incapable of living and acting, all
the more do interior maturity and spiritual greatness
become evident, constituting a touching loss to those
who are healthy and normal.

Suffering is a grace not only to the one invited into it but
to those around the person as well: relatives, friends, health
care workers. Human suffering can evoke compassion and
respect in those sensitive enough to resonate to it — and,
even before that, willing enough to experience it. Think of
the reluctance we feel about visiting a friend in a hospital or
nursing home; think of the aversion many young people have
at the beginning of their first service project. Jesus came to
heal us of that withholding, too. The call of their need can
be a redemptive occasion for us, too.

According to Jesus' picture of the Last Judgment, there
is only *one* issue in God's appraisal of whether each of us
fulfilled the stewardship of our lives: "I was hungry and you
gave me food; I was thirsty and you gave me drink; I was a
stranger and you made me welcome; naked and you clothed
me, sick and you visited me, in prison and you came to see

me" (Mt 25:35–36). That is the only value at stake in judging your life: compassion.

As Kurt Vonnegut's Eliot Rosewater put it far more tersely: "There's only one commandment: Goddammit, you've got to be kind."

Letting Go

Here and there, in order to anchor the inquiry into suffering in the everydays of our lives, I've fallen back on my own experience: the suffering I know best. I ask indulgence for doing so again, better to understand what metanoia means.

Perhaps the greatest invitation suffering offered me, outside my suicidal depression in theology, more painful even than my parents' deaths, was when I discovered in a totally unexpected letter that I was being transferred (notice the passive verb) from a place I had served with all my heart and soul for twenty-two years. I was doing work I loved, in a place I loved, with people I loved, and I had more than enough evidence to be sure they loved me as well. It came without warning, although superiors insisted discernment had been going on for three years without my realizing.

I received divorce papers after twenty-two years, no reasons. Oh, and by the way, you're now married to this woman you've never met down in the Bronx. My two closest friends offered all they possibly could: the anguish in their eyes. But I was encased in an isolation even the truest friend could not enter or share.

Since that wondrous event before ordination when I knew without question I was a good man, not because of who I was but because I had been accepted, I'd become *too* confident. I found I was too busy to pray. For quite a few years, I "didn't need it." But when I read that letter, my knees were literally quaking. I couldn't support myself. That's when I was "hurled" back into the wilderness to begin praying again. I had no choice.

I used a lot of words at first. "Oh, God, no! Oh, please don't let this be true!" Denial. For a couple of days, all I could do was cry. Then on my retreat I was suddenly "steered" to confront Abraham, ordered by God to sacrifice what he loved best in the whole world. And God seemed to be saying to me, "Do you really love me best? Or Isaac?" The answer was obvious: Isaac.

That same evening I was steered yet again to (of all things) an old joke: A mountain climber is alone, approaching the very peak, when suddenly he slips and slithers through the gravel to the edge. But he manages to grab hold of a tough bush rooted at the edge. "Help!" he cries. "Is there anybody up there?" A booming voice answers, "This is God! Let go! I'll catch you!" And the poor chap wrenches around and cries out, "Is there anybody *else* up there?" I heard God inside my soul whispering, "Let go! I'll catch you!" There was nobody else. So I surrendered Isaac. I let go. And God caught me.

I'll never get back anyone like Isaac, as Abraham did. I'll never get my children back, as Job did. But I did rise painfully from soul-death, as Jesus did. I couldn't have, without him.

Soul-Making

St. Irenaeus believed the purpose of human life is soul-making. In fact, one might say that, because God is surely restless and uncomfortable with stasis, the whole creation since the beginning has been groaning toward soul-making: giving birth to life out of inanimate matter, then giving birth to the life of movement and feeling, then giving birth to understanding life — to the soul, without which life is value-less, the aimless coping of animals with an unacknowledged and unevolved human potential. Then finally, in the fullness of time, came Jesus the Christ, the definitive final stage of evolution, inviting us to fusion with — and the infusion of — divine life. He offers an invitation to live not just within ourselves but to live within his Spirit.

Jesus said, "The Kingdom of God is very near to you" (Lk 10:11), not just after life but here and now. If what Jesus says is true, God participates in every event in our lives, great or small. As Daniel Liderbach writes:

> The foundation for living in the spirit is that God is present and active within every experience. The individuals who are sensitive and responsive to their spirits, therefore, are sensitive and responsive to God and to the kingdom of God. This is quite a different sensitivity and responsibility from being conventionally religious.

Genuine religion means a person-to-Person *connection*. It need have nothing whatever to do with Christianity or Catholicism, nothing to do with intricate theologies, nothing to do with ritual. All those can amplify and enrich the connection which is religion, but they don't constitute it. In fact, without the connection, all of the rest is either vacuous or pretentious or both. What Job and Jesus clung to in their near despair was that connection.

If there's a purgatory (and I suspect there must be, though hardly Dante's), it's most likely a remedial course, where we finally learn what's truly important, what life was all about, what success really means — when we could have learned it here.

'Twas ever thus. Seniors sneer when I tell them they could learn in high school what they will most probably have to spend five times more money to learn in college. Husbands reaching their middle years leave wives and families "to find myself," when they could and should have discovered an identity in adolescence. Too many of us won't be ready for heaven, not because we're burdened with sins to be purged, but because we've been blind to the truth of human purpose all along.

Try to envision a world *without* suffering, disequilibriums, challenges, crises. Orwell tried; Huxley tried. B. F. Skinner tried to take us to a world *beyond* freedom and dignity, a world in which there was no crime, no moral evil rooted in inhuman motives — but also a world in which so much we revere could not exist: compassion, courage, determination, integrity, heroism. Without suffering, there could be no stories. How can one achieve anything if fulfillment is simply a given? In such a world without suffering, Socrates could not exist, nor Jeremiah, nor Job, nor the Maccabees, nor Jesus, nor Peter, nor the martyrs of the arena, nor Joan of Arc,

Thomas More, Abraham Lincoln, Albert Schweitzer, Helen Keller, Dorothy Day, Tom Dooley, Martin Luther King, Jr., Nelson Mandela, Terry Anderson, the heroes and heroines of the camps.

In such a world, Bill Fold would have been incapable of greatness. So would we all.

 # Epilogue

My mother died in January 1981. To be honest, I can't remember the date. That seems as callous as Meursault in *The Stranger*, but there had been so many "deaths."

Another Jesuit in the community, Vin McDonough, usually got up in the early hours to grade papers in the quiet. He got the call at about 4:30, but with his usual sensitivity realized there was no value in telling me then. So at 7:30 he knocked on the door, and I looked up at him. "It's Mom, isn't it," I asked. And he nodded.

I couldn't grasp it, not the way I took the stunning news my dad had dropped dead in the street on his way to a prayer rally. I felt what a fighter must feel when the ref finally calls the fight in the middle of an uncountable round, and the blows just...stop. Or like the prisoners on the last day of Dachau when the howitzers suddenly fell silent.

I called Bill Murphy, the Buffalo funeral director who had helped with both of my aunts' funerals. I told him I wanted no wake; Mom had been out of circulation for eight years, unreachable for three; most of her closest friends and all her siblings were dead. I asked for the tiny chapel which had been the first church in our parish before the new big colonial one. It had been built by John Neumann, who later became Bishop of Philadelphia and even later a canonized saint. Mom and Dad had been among the first couples in the parish and pitched in to clean, paint, and polish it when it was reopened. It was "hers," and it was also small; there'd probably be few there. And I insisted on a closed casket. Bill agreed to it all, for the moment.

Foolishly, I suppose, I told no one in the community or the school. I guess I didn't want to be pitied; perhaps it was that I still didn't honestly believe it was true. I taught class; I directed a rehearsal of *Oklahoma;* then I drove to Buffalo as I had so many, many Sundays, but this time for the last time.

Next morning, my sister and I arrived at the funeral home to give Mom the last blessing before going to the church. Bill Murphy told me he felt very strongly we ought to let him open the coffin so we could see Mom one last time. I gritted my teeth against it, but some more redeemed part of me grasped that he'd had much more experience of bereavement than I. So I said yes. He went inside and opened it, then called us in.

I was amazed. Mom looked beautiful! For years she had let her hair go: the girls were too snippy, the driers were too hot, the curl fell out in a week anyway. Now, her hair was snow white, crimped and waved. And her face was finally at peace.

Years of dealing with death and sharing sorrow had made Bill Murphy wise.

The tiny church was packed. Friends I hadn't seen in years. At least a dozen Jesuits from Rochester and Buffalo and even Syracuse. I still had a great many things to learn.

I began the homily I'd worked on all the previous evening with real confidence. But when I got to the very end, I quoted Martin Luther King, looking down at the cold box that held my doorway into life. "Free at last," I said, "free at last. Thank God Almigh-..." I choked, my jaws working against it. But I finally got it out: "Thank God Almighty, she's free at last!"

Love isn't a feeling. It's an act of the will. But some-times — the best times — love's a feeling, too.

OF RELATED INTEREST